Raising Children in a Socially Toxic Environment

James Garbarino

Raising
Children
in a
Socially Toxic
Environment

Jossey-Bass Publishers • San Francisco

FIRST PAPERBACK EDITION PUBLISHED IN 1999.

Jossey-Bass books and products are available through most bookstores. To contact Jossey-Bass directly, call (888) 378-2537, fax to (800) 605-2665, or visit our website at www.josseybass.com.

Substantial discounts on bulk quantities of Jossey-Bass books are available to corporations, professional associations, and other organizations. For details and discount information, contact the special sales department at Jossey-Bass Inc., Publishers.

 Manufactured in the United States of America on Lyons Falls Turin Book. This paper is acid-free and 100 percent totally chlorine-free.

Library of Congress Cataloging-in-Publication Data

Garbarino, James.
    Raising children in a socially toxic environment / James Garbarino.
        p.   cm.
    Includes bibliographical references and index.
    ISBN 0-7879-0116-4 (hardcover)
    ISBN 0-7879-5042-4 (paperback)
    1. Child rearing.   2. Social problems.   I. Title.
HQ769.G258   1995
649'.1—dc20   95-20428

FIRST EDITION
HB Printing   10 9 8 7 6 5
PB Printing   10 9 8 7 6 5 4 3 2

Contents

For Claire, my soulmate

Preface

When I was in high school in the 1960s, I used to write an opinion column for the school newspaper. One month I wrote an article criticizing the fraternities at my school, an act that angered many of my peers. As a result, late one night a car pulled up and dumped garbage on the lawn of our house: I was the victim of a drive-by *littering*.

Today, in many communities, the consequence of making your adolescent peers mad at you might be a drive-by *shooting* instead of a pile of garbage on your lawn. The same behavior that thirty years ago produced a rather benign form of intimidation might today get you killed. This insight started me thinking about the many ways in which the social environment for kids today is more dangerous than it was when I was growing up. *Drugs:* There was no crack cocaine available to troubled kids then. *Violence:* It was almost unheard of for a teenage bully to have a gun. *AIDS:* We were warned off sex, but no one said we would die from it. *Television:* The content of television programs was bland and innocuous by today's standards. *Family instability:* Most families had two parents and could afford to live on one income.

These thoughts led me to the concept of the socially toxic environment, the idea that the mere act of living in our society today is dangerous to the health and well-being of children and adolescents. As I see it, in the past thirty to forty years we have witnessed a deterioration of the quality of social life that has profound implications for child development, particularly for children and youth whose personality, temperament, and life experiences make them especially vulnerable. This social deterioration is related to the changing nature of our economy. It also is related to the growing dependence of families on the community for support, and to the increasing nastiness of the culture in which children live.

The actual writing of this book began with a keynote address delivered to the National PTA Congress in June 1992. In that address, I gave voice to my previously uncoordinated concerns and fears for children, youth, and families. Since then I have been exploring these issues with citizens, parents, and professionals throughout North America. And wherever I have gone, I have found resonance with my concerns. Some communities feel they are in the throes of a social toxicity crisis—with teenagers falling victim to the violence and nastiness in droves. Other communities feel they are starting down the same road and are looking for guidance in how to turn back from what they see happening elsewhere.

My hope is that this book will help individuals and groups throughout North America work together to detoxify the social environment *and* to strengthen kids and parents to resist those toxic influences that cannot be changed in the short run. It's an ambitious goal. I realize that. But I have great confidence in the human capacity for action.

I have seen brave individuals organize their neighbors to "take back the streets" and demonstrate to alienated youth that adults can be trusted to take charge of their communities so kids can be kids. I have seen dedicated parents find ways to communicate strong positive values to their children, values that are backed up with commitment of the most precious gift—time together in constructive activities. I have seen what a difference it makes to a single parent to have a supportive community—one that provides safe and affordable child care. I have seen parents taking a stand against the nastiness and emptiness of modern consumer culture—turning off the TV, taking a walk with their children rather than leaving them to video games, teaching by example a norm of gentleness and good manners. I have visited socially supportive communities—throwbacks to an earlier era when neighborhoods and towns really did offer a "kinder and gentler" America.

Over the last decade, I have also visited war zones and impoverished communities all over the world—meeting community leaders and parents in dire circumstances who have refused to give in to desperation. These experiences convinced me that if we are open to cultural innovation we can make things work better for children and youth. This is a message of hope.

I find myself thinking of Charles Dickens's A *Christmas Carol*, in which Ebenezer Scrooge is shown his past, present, and future by helpful spirits. When all is done, he asks the spirit if the images of the future he has been shown are those that *might* be or those that *must* be. Like the spirit in Dickens's story, I say that what I will show the reader is not written in stone. This is only the story of what might be, but it will come to pass if we do not act with a passion to make a difference.

In the following chapters, I begin by establishing a picture of what childhood ought to be, if well-grown and civil adults are to emerge from it, and then describe the way in which children map their own worlds and thus define themselves. Then, chapter by chapter, I analyze the needs we must meet because they are essential to our children's well-being. These needs are stability, security, affirmation and acceptance, family time, values and connection to community, and access to basic resources. The degree to which we meet these needs shapes our children's social maps, their behavior, and their hope for the future—in other words, the degree to which they will thrive. I suggest the forms these needs take, the ways in which the socially toxic environment now fails to meet these needs—substituting violence, nastiness, insecurity, isolation, and poverty in their place—and some of the ways parents and citizens and teachers can start changing the environment both at home and in the wider society.

Policy makers, parents, professionals, spiritual leaders, and concerned citizens can make a difference. I cannot believe anything else.

Acknowledgments

The writing of this book was aided by many colleagues, friends, and family members around the world. My colleagues at Cornell University and the Family Life Development Center offered help in finishing my rough thoughts. Dr. Jed Weitzen played a special role in the final stages, offering personal and professional kindness and support at a difficult time. My global network of colleagues "in the field" and in academic institutions offered inspiration and information. My colleague at Erikson Institute, Kathleen Kostelny, provided helpful suggestions at many points in the process and bibliographic assistance throughout. My secretary at Erikson, Norma Richman, assisted in the preparation of the manuscript. The insights of Claire Bedard and the editors at Jossey-Bass did wonders in helping bring my thoughts into a more coherent voice. The many journalists, parents, policy makers, and professionals in the field who spoke with me—asking questions that stimulated me to write this book as an answer—all contributed. Members of my family, past and present, listened and provoked. I thank and appreciate them all, especially my two children, Josh and Joanna, from whom I have learned much. Special thanks to the Centre Avenue Elementary School and East Rockaway High School in East Rockaway, New York, where I spent my childhood and youth and learned how to be a person. Particular thanks to my peers in the class of '64, with whom I forged an identity. Thanks to the faculty and students of St. Lawrence University, where I learned to be a scholar, and to Cornell University, where I learned to be a professional.

But one presence must be acknowledged above all others: Urie Bronfenbrenner. For nearly thirty years, Urie has been my mentor and friend. In many ways this book is his intellectual grandchild. His classic *Two Worlds of Childhood*[1] inspired and guided me as a graduate student, and anyone familiar with it will see that inspiration reflected in *Raising Children in a Socially Toxic Environment*. I thank, honor, and cherish him, and offer this book to him as an act of love.

Ithaca, New York   James Garbarino
June 1995

The Author

James Garbarino is codirector of the Family Life Development Center and professor of human development at Cornell University in Ithaca, New York. From 1985 to 1994, prior to coming to Cornell, he served as president of the Erikson Institute for Advanced Study in Child Development in Chicago, Illinois. He has studied the impact of violence and stress on children and youth throughout North America and around the world, and is the author of seventeen books, including *The Psychologically Battered Child* (1986), *What Children Can Tell Us* (1989), *No Place to Be a Child: Growing Up in a War Zone* (1991), *Children and Families in the Social Environment* (1992), *Children in Danger: Coping with the Consequences of Community Violence* (1992), and *Lost Boys: Why Our Sons Turn Violent and How We Can Save Them* (1999). In 1989, he received the American Psychological Association's Award for Distinguished Professional Contributions to Public Service, and in 1995, the Dale Richmond Award from the American Academy of Pediatrics. He has served as a consultant to a wide range of organizations, including the American Medical Association and the National Committee to Prevent Child Abuse. He is a father and stepfather of teenage children.

Raising Children in a
Socially Toxic Environment

Chapter One

What Childhood Ought to Be

When I talk with American teachers who have been in the field since the 1950s, I often ask them to identify the kinds of discipline problems they used to face. Here's what they come up with: gum chewing, talking back, disorder in the halls, making a mess in the classroom, dress-code violations, and being noisy. When I talk to today's teachers and ask them the same question, their lists read like a police blotter: violence against self and others, substance abuse, robbery, and sexual victimization.[1] Things have changed.

Some of this difference between now and then simply reflects today's greater awareness of problems. When I was in high school, there certainly were kids using drugs and alcohol. Girls did get pregnant. Child abuse did exist. But for the most part, we didn't know about it. Looking back with the benefit of hindsight, I realize that, as kids, we were shielded from knowing some of these things by adults who thought we would be better off not knowing. Some of the change is therefore a change in awareness all around: Adults today are more conscious of the problems children and youth encounter, and they more readily let children and youth in on what's going on. The child abuse problem illustrates this change. Increased professional and public awareness in the 1970s and 1980s led to skyrocketing rates of reported child maltreatment. At the same time, widespread efforts were being launched to inform children at large about the risks they faced from potentially abusive adults.

Interestingly, there is often a weak connection between how people perceive the social environment and its actual reality. For example, while the number of homicides in Miami decreased from 1982 to 1992 (by 5 percent, according to one source), 73 percent of Miamians surveyed by NBC News said they thought homicide rates had increased during that period. Only 3 percent realized the rates had decreased. In this case, it seems that the news media's highlighting of murders in that community had elevated popular awareness and led to the misperception.[2]

Having said that, I think the current situation is more complex than a simple combination of greater awareness and better reporting. For instance, Fordham University's Institute for Social Policy produces an Index of Social Health for the United States, based upon sixteen measures including infant mortality, teenage suicide, dropout rates, drug abuse, homicide, food stamp use, unemployment, traffic deaths, and poverty among the elderly. The index ranges between 0 and 100 (with 100 being the best). From 1970 to 1992, the index showed a decline from 74 to 41.[3] This means that the overall well-being of our society decreased significantly.

The Problem Is Real

Kids today are in trouble, more trouble than they were when I was growing up. Evidence of this is found in research on emotional and behavioral problems among American children.

The most compelling study of this change used a tool called the Child Behavior Checklist. Tom Achenbach developed this survey questionnaire in an attempt to identify a wide range of emotional and behavioral problems from a list of 113 specific items. This assessment instrument is widely used in research in the United States and in other countries. Parents (or other adults who know the child well) indicate the presence (or absence) and intensity of each of the 113 specific behaviors or feelings in words such as "can't sit still, restless, or hyperactive," "lying or cheating," "feels worthless or inferior," "cruelty, bullying or meanness to others," and "nervous, high-strung, or tense."

Since 1974, 45 of the 113 problems have become significantly worse.[4] Negative feelings such as apathy, sadness, and various forms of distress have increased. Moreover, children report disliking school more. To some extent, this difference may result from greater awareness on the part of parents and teachers (the ones likely to fill out the survey). But it's more than just that.

In 1976, 3 percent of the children studied were seeing therapists. By 1989, that percentage had grown to 8 percent. Greater awareness of problems may play a partial role in this, too, but there is more to it. In 1976, 10 percent of all children studied were judged to be doing so poorly that they could be candidates for therapy (even though only a third of these kids actually received such therapy). By 1989, 18 percent of the children were doing badly enough in their behavior and development to warrant needing therapy (and about half were getting it). Both analyses are based on samples of children from the general population, not those in psychiatric institutions. Thus, if anything, they underestimate the number of kids in trouble because they exclude the most troubled kids, the ones already in therapy.

Achenbach's data certainly conform to the observations of teachers and other professionals who work with children. On many occasions in the last few years, I have had an opportunity to ask those who have worked with children professionally for thirty years or more what they have observed. They overwhelmingly see what Achenbach has observed in his data: more and more children are in greater and greater trouble. And it's not just children. Survey data on depression indicate that the proportion of people who experience a major problem with depression (making them unable to meet their normal responsibilities) by age thirty-five has increased from 16 percent in 1950 to 40 percent in 1990. For children under age fifteen, the change is from 1.5 percent in 1950 to 8 percent in 1979.

This is one indicator of how difficult it is to grow up these days. As greater numbers of our children display signs of experiencing

serious problems we have to ask, Why? My own answer to this question is that I think it is because children today live in a socially
toxic environment. I also think children are most vulnerable to the
negative influence of a socially toxic environment, and that unless
we do something about it now, the situation for children will only
continue to deteriorate.

The Concept of the "Socially Toxic Environment"

What I mean by the term *socially toxic environment* is that the social world of children, the social context in which they grow up,
has become poisonous to their development. I offer this term as a
parallel to the environmental movement's analysis regarding physical toxicity as a threat to human well-being and survival. The
nature of physical toxicity is now well known and is a matter for
public policy and private concern. For example, we now know that
the declining sperm count of American males throughout the twentieth century is a result of the buildup of toxic substances in the
physical environment—in the air, the water, the soil. And we know
that air quality is a major problem in many places, so much so that
in some cities, just breathing "normally" is a threat to your health.[5]

In the last ten years, some places have improved the quality of
their physical environment, as public and professional awareness
has led to changes. In the matter of recognizing, understanding, and
reversing social toxicity, however, we lag far behind. We don't have
a direct social equivalent to *Silent Spring*, Rachel Carson's landmark
analysis of physical toxicity.[6] Her book, first published in 1953,
called attention to the problem and stimulated reforms that led to
public action to ban DDT and move against many of the most
severe manifestations of physical toxicity in the environment.
Nonetheless, we still need to deal with the social equivalents of lead
and smoke in the air, PCBs in the water, and pesticides in the food
chain. They're easy enough to identify: violence, poverty and other
economic pressures on parents and their children, disruption of rela-

tionships, nastiness, despair, depression, paranoia, alienation—all the things that demoralize families and communities. These are the forces in the land that pollute the environment of children and youth. These are the elements of social toxicity.

Social life is more risky now than it was just forty years ago; the level of social and cultural poison is higher. How is the environment for kids more socially toxic now than it was when I was a child? For one thing, no kid ever died from a drive-by fist fight, but the proliferation of guns among growing numbers of adolescent peer groups means that conflict and confrontations that once were settled with fists now can lead to shooting. The drive-by littering I experienced when I angered my classmates in 1963 was radically different from the threat faced today by a teen who crosses his or her peers.

Kids today are bombarded with messages about the potentially lethal consequences of sex. There is no comparison between the threat of AIDS today and the threat of VD during my youth. More generally, children and youth today must contend with a constant stream of messages that undermine their sense of security. If it isn't the threat of kidnapping, it's the high probability of parental divorce. If it isn't weapons at school, it's contemplating a future with dim employment opportunities.

But beyond these dramatic issues there are more, many more, that are subtle yet equally serious. High on the list is the departure of adults from the lives of kids. The lack of adult supervision and time spent doing constructive, cooperative activities are important toxic aspects of the social environment today, and compound the effects of other negative influences in the social environment for kids. Kids home alone are more vulnerable to every cultural poison they encounter than they would be if backed up by adults.

Although everyone is vulnerable to toxicity in the social environment, children are the most vulnerable, just as they are among the most vulnerable to physical toxicity in the environment. When airborne pollution gets really bad, it is the children with asthma or other respiratory conditions who show the effects soonest and with greatest intensity. When a house is contaminated with lead or asbestos, the youngest children are at greatest risk.

This analogy leads to one of the central elements of my message: As the social environment becomes more toxic, it is the children—particularly the most vulnerable among them—who show the effects first and worst. And the children who will show the effects of social toxicity first and most dramatically are the ones who have accumulated the most developmental risk factors. These children already stand on the edge of life's abyss. Their risk factors are the stuff of talk shows and headlines and policy seminars: absent fathers, poverty and other economic pressures, racism, addiction, educational failure, poor physical health, family violence, and adult emotional problems that impair parenting. Each of these factors multiplies the effects of any others that may be present, and so risk accumulates.[7] The children's vulnerability to social toxicity increases. Social toxicity undermines their self-confidence and feelings of self-worth. It squanders opportunities for positive experiences that might give them strength. It erodes childhood itself.

What Is Childhood?

In order to understand fully what is happening to our children, we need a view of what childhood ought to be. What does it mean to be a child? Perhaps it is a sign of the times that I feel a need to ask such a question. In earlier times, and in other places around the world even today, the question would seem silly. The answer would be obvious. "This is a child," the respondent might say, pointing to the example nearest at hand. I'm sure if you had asked my parents in the 1950s when I was growing up they would have responded that way.

But to us here and now, the question is a real one, and one that needs answering, particularly among the middle class, the class that leads the way in defining what is good and normal in our society.

And, like most of the things about life in middle-class modern North America, our uncertainty about the meaning of being a child is both good and bad. It is good because it means we are engaged in a debate about children and childhood.

Some societies would not bother. In some societies, people still buy and sell children or ruthlessly exploit their labor—and let's not forget that this also happens in the dark corners of our own society. Case closed. The young are simply the disposable property of parents and other adults.

But because our society is engaged in a process of debate and reflection about childhood, we have the prospect of moving to more humane and empathetic ways of caring for our children. We can find better ways to be parents than we currently practice.

On the other hand, the fact that we are asking about the meaning of childhood is bad too. It shows that as a society we lack a shared definition of children and childhood, leaving every man, woman, and child to try to figure out things that used to be part of the social atmosphere. And so we ask, what time should young people go to bed? What time should young people come home when they are out with their friends? What is the age to start having sex? To bear children? What is the age to be left without adult supervision for long periods? What is the age to learn to read? What is the age to start working for money outside the home? What is the age to start school? Day care? Self care? What is the age to do X, Y, and Z? I ask and answer those questions publicly all the time in my professional work—and then again privately as a parent. And the fact that all of these matters are questions debated every day in newspaper advice columns, parent meetings, classrooms, and talk shows signifies that we have no clear consensus about children and childhood.

Nevertheless, there are signs of an emerging global consensus about the meaning of childhood. I see this in the international discussion and validation of the United Nations Convention on the Rights of the Child. The U.N. Convention is an effort to express a universal definition of what it should mean to be a child, a universal definition based on what middle-class societies have learned about children and child development. (I say what it *should* mean because words in documents don't necessarily stand for facts in reality.) I believe that this definition can supply a large part of the perspective on childhood that we need if we are to be better parents to our own children and better advocates for all children. It can suggest what we would like to achieve for our children and what kind of childhood we want them to enjoy.

The U.N. Convention on the Rights of the Child is a long and complicated document,[8] but at its heart it proposes that to be a child is to be shielded from the direct demands of adult economic, political, and sexual forces. It proclaims that childhood is a protected niche in the social environment, a special time and place in the human life cycle, having a special claim on the community. Regardless of their economic value, children have a right to receive support from their families and communities. They have a right to be shielded from war and violence, to lead a life free from adult sexuality, and to have a positive identity both as individuals and as part of a group.

The U.N. Convention embodies one of the basic principles of middle-class family life: it tells us that children need not pay their own way and earn their keep. They have a human right to be cared for. Typically, families want to provide this support, and as a rule, they will do so if possible. But when families cannot provide for their children, the U.N. Convention tells us that society should pick up the tab, that children have economic rights. This deeply held principle gives moral force to ongoing efforts to eliminate exploitive labor and poverty from the lives of children. And specific articles in the U.N. Convention testify to this impetus to offer every child what middle-class families offer to their children. We should bear this in mind in our own society, where we see a high and growing rate of poverty among children.[9]

But the economic foundations of childhood go beyond simple protection from poverty. The idea of childhood as a protected niche implies that children are not direct participants in the cash economy. If they work, their work is guided, under the protection of their parents, and (it is to be hoped) in the service of educational and developmental purposes. We can celebrate the strides that have been made here and elsewhere in protecting children from workforce participation. Dramatically reducing child labor was an important accomplishment in creating childhood in the United States, and around the world it remains a hot issue. But the economic rights of children go beyond being protected from adult work.

The child also has a right to be protected from the excesses of the consumer economy. In this view, the child's own purchases are to be kept separate and sheltered from commercial advertising that exploits the cognitive, emotional, and social limitations of children. Failure to provide such shielding is a violation of their rights—and it happens over and over. Turn on a television set during the children's hours before and after school, on weekends, and in the early evening, and you can see for yourself where our society stands on this matter. Children are commercial targets. Walk around any shopping mall, and you can see today's parents trying to cope with the fruits of this commercial exploitation of childhood. You may well be one of these parents. I know I am.

In addition to the economic protections afforded children in the U.N. Convention, there are political rights as well. The most important of these is to stand in a privileged position with respect to government. Children cannot vote, are not legally accountable (except in special circumstances when they can be tried in adult courts for especially violent offenses) and are not expected to be used by competing political forces in society. And yet government has obligations toward children. They are to receive special protection in case of war and community violence. They are entitled to special treatment if they are harmed as collateral damage in an armed conflict. Articles 38 and 39 address these issues explicitly and directly: children are off-limits during times of war and entitled to special rehabilitation if they are affected adversely.

Beyond war, children are to be protected from violence in general. The U.N. Convention prohibits the execution of minors. It urges that parents and teachers adopt a nonviolent approach to discipline. This is very much in keeping with the evolution of professional understanding of child development. More and more middle-class adults around the world have come to see the validity of this insight and thus to acknowledge that "children are not for hitting." As a result of this growing awareness, schools ban corporal punishment and parents seek alternatives to spanking and beating children. Child development research and human rights go hand in hand here.

Imagine telling children they must earn their dinners or their parents' interest on the basis of their accomplishments, of what they do. No. Children are to have their food and the regard of their parents because of the fact of their relationship, of who they are. More broadly, as I will show later, children need to relate to adults on a person-to-person basis, as individuals and not as categories. Some years ago, sociologist Jacob Getzels referred to this difference as being between a *particularistic* (who you are) and a *universalistic* (what you do) orientation.[10] We ought to view childhood as a time to maximize the particularistic and minimize the universalistic.

Besides being economically privileged and politically protected, children are supposed to be off-limits to adult sexuality. They are not sex objects. In their behavior, their interests, their attitudes, and their bodies, they are off-limits. Children require protection from adult sexual experiences.

In modern Western societies, this principle used to be reinforced by the distinctly different clothing worn by children. Little more than fifty years ago, boys wore short pants until adolescence as a symbol of their childhood status. For girls, accoutrements of fashion such as makeup and stockings were part of the adolescent rite of passage. Clothing once differentiated children from adolescents and adults, and symbolized their being off-limits sexually (which is not to say that this principle—and children themselves—were not violated). Today, even young children wear clothing undifferentiated from that worn by teenagers and grownups. Visiting the children's section of a department store recently reminded me of this change. The only difference between the styles for boys and girls on the one hand, and adults, on the other, is size. Children were certainly subjected to sexual abuse before the change in clothing took place. But I suggest that the change shows how we are failing to recognize childhood as a special time that is very different from adulthood. Dressing children like adults sends a message.

To be sure, children are physical, even sensual creatures. But they are not sexual unless corrupted by adults or adolescents. Although some kids are more physical than others, children generally respond well to physical affection. It's more than that, really. Children need physical affection to thrive emotionally, so much so that kids who are deprived of this affection are put in jeopardy. Ironically, these children may even be at greater risk of being sexually abused by predatory adults who appreciate this unmet need and exploit it seductively. As David Finkelhor makes clear in his analysis of sexual abuse,[11] children are not in a position, developmentally or socially, to give informed consent for sexual involvements. They lack the cognitive and emotional equipment to figure out the consequences. Also, they lack the independent status necessary to decide freely: in any interaction between a child and an adult there is the presumption of adult authority. When children are involved, there can be no liaison between consenting persons. Children cannot say No with sufficient authority and awareness. Therefore, they are prohibited from saying Yes, just as adults are prohibited from asking.

The Purpose of Childhood

I believe that we ought to view childhood as a social space in which to lay the foundation for the best that human development has to offer. And if we are to be successful parents in a socially toxic environment, we must understand that children develop largely through play. As Maria Montessori put it, "play is the child's work." The purpose of play is to provide a social context for children in which each can bear the fruits of human evolution.[12]

Children are shielded so that they can play, and this play is quintessentially human. Jacob Bronowski correctly recognized this when he spoke of the human being's "long childhood" as a key to the cultural ascent of our species.[13] As he saw it, childhood is both the cause and consequence of cultural evolution. As a species, we have evolved culturally in large part because of our playfulness, and all that it produces in the way of intelligence and creativity. We have made a social space for play because our culture can subsidize childhood as a time for free play.

The child is given license to play, and in so doing to explore the world. This play is distinguished from adult labor in that it doesn't have production as its goal, although work can be an important activity for children. Child's play is distinguished from adult games in that it isn't a basis for courtship, even though children do have romantic relationships. This play is free, but the payoffs are enormous.

In the summer months, my children have been fortunate to be able to spend their time in a rural setting, alongside a small lake that flows out into a small river. The other children who inhabit this environment are often seen at play in this free way. They putter around in boats. They build elaborate camps on the shore. They try to catch fish, water bugs, and other creatures of the field and stream. They do nothing.

And when I see them I am reminded of a marvelous children's book that conveys the wisdom of such free play, *How Tom Beat*

Captain Najork and His Hired Sportsmen.[14] In this book, young Tom is a master of fooling around. In the eyes of his domineering Aunt, he is wasting time, however, and she calls upon Captain Najork to teach the boy a lesson about the importance of buckling down, by challenging him to a series of games of the Captain's choosing. But as the story reveals, through his free play Tom has been assembling the skills and attitudes he will need to master the challenges of Captain Najork's games—and for that matter, of life. It's a wise book. Too many parents and teachers have lost that wisdom. They permit children to wallow in the passive wasteland of television or hurry children to lessons and other organized activities in the name of creating "learning experiences." Play becomes work, and this contributes to the social toxicity of the environment for children.

Child's play is geared to fantasy as a vehicle for processing experiences, testing hypotheses about the self and the world, and having fun. It also provides a domain in which adults and children can communicate in a way that facilitates the child's development, if adults accept the child's definition of the play's reality. Vivian Paley is one educator who knows this.[15] She has built her curriculum around the play and stories of young children. Her observations of what happens offer the adult a glimpse into the child's world. In that world, children play. Through their play, they come to live better. They figure things out. They learn. They become more fully human.

I do not mean to imply that the world of children is just fun and games. Quite the contrary, childhood can be a very serious proposition, as is clear if you watch youngsters learning to tie their shoes, figuring out how to come to terms with the death of a pet dog, or trying to make sense of divorce. As children do such things, they develop basic competence. This is the second purpose of childhood.

Children must become adept at the basic skills of the human community in which they live. These skills extend to everything from learning how to talk, to becoming toilet trained, to learning how to work, to becoming a moral person. Unless children become competent in these areas they are a problem—for their family, for their society, and for themselves. Cultures may differ in what they expect (for example, learning to read in England versus caring for the land in the highlands of Guatemala), but everywhere children are expected to learn the ropes. Childhood is thus a period of social-ization, of adult investment in the creation of socially relevant skills, beliefs, and motives: "As the twig's inclined, so the tree is bent."

Play and developing competence go together, of course. For the child, they are at the top of life's agenda. Identifying opportunities for children to become socialized through play is an important func-tion for teachers, parents, coaches, and artists. It takes time and a willingness to trust the child. Many adults too easily panic at the thought that play goes nowhere, leads nowhere, accomplishes noth-ing. They often wonder, "When will the kid get down to business?" So, for example, they may preempt the natural order of childhood things and seek to teach children to read before those children are really ready to join the literate community. Societies differ in this matter, too. For example, British children are expected to read by age five; in Sweden, it is age seven. The result of premature pres-sure to read is often less reading in the long run, however. By the time they are ten, children taught to read too early read no better than other children, and they read less on their own, for pleasure.[16]

Learning about the world through free play and learning skills at a child's pace as one is ready for them requires a lengthy childhood, and it often seems that we have become impatient with that childhood. I'm told that the Swiss psychologist Jean Piaget recalled that when he first began to visit and lecture in the United States about the stages of development, the first question he was always asked was how to speed up the process, how to stim-ulate quicker movement from the lower to the higher stages. "Why are you Americans always in such a hurry?" he responded. Why indeed? Why are we in such a hurry to have girls look like little women? Why are we in such a hurry to have child athletes partic-ipate in organized competitive sports? Why are we so eager to squander childhood, one of the greatest accomplishments of human evolution? Perhaps our shortsightedness in this matter parallels the problems we face in our economic system, where short-term gain is often pursued at the expense of long-term investment.

A Precious Accomplishment

Childhood is about being free to play and learn and love, being safe from the pressures of adult economic and sexual forces, and being accepted for who you are and not what you do. It is about being party to an implicit social contract in which adults promise to honor and cherish, and children promise to obey and learn. This is childhood in its best sense, a sense that has emerged over several centuries of trial and error, largely as a result of middle-class cultural innovation.

The concept of childhood I have been describing didn't come out of nowhere. It required some rather dramatic and important economic and social developments. It also required a significant shift in the demography of children.[17] Before there could be a protected childhood, there had to be an assumption that a child would survive into adulthood to justify the parents' investment. Only when infant mortality rates were reduced from hundreds per thousand to tens per thousand, and the proportion of children dying before age five dropped from roughly 50 percent (in medieval times) to about 10 percent (during the industrial revolution) could we reasonably think of offering our children childhood as a cultural experience.

But it took more than demography to create childhood as I've been describing it. It also took the emergence of middle-class society, with its emphasis on literacy, schooling, and deliberate child development, coupled with the affluence necessary to underwrite the costs of providing these experiences to children. Thus, childhood as a protected time and space in the human life course has always been related to social class.[18] It ebbs and flows as the economic situation of families changes, particularly as the middle class grows or shrinks. It depends upon our being able to subsidize adults to educate and teach children, and upon our being able to free children from adult responsibilities in order to play.

In short, bringing the concept of childhood to fruition required dramatic decreases in infant mortality, insight into the possibilities of human nature, allocation of resources to subsidize schooling and play time, and knowledge about the processes of child development. What is it worth, this middle-class concept of childhood?

I believe this concept is more than just nostalgia or soft-headed wishful thinking. It is a bit of hard-headed social analysis to recognize middle-class childhood as something of enormous value, for its developmental utility and for its social importance. Therefore, it is the rationale for everything else that comes later in this book.

I use this concept of childhood as a standard with which to evaluate the social environment of children. In other words, one way we know an environment is becoming socially toxic is when we observe an erosion of middle-class childhood. Childhood is the measuring stick for assessing social changes (intended or incidental) that encroach upon the lives of children and parents. Although the middle-class form of childhood appeared first as a kind of cultural luxury (when the middle class was tiny), it has proved to be a sound investment. Looking at it now, we can see that it has long-term payoffs for the individual and for the society. But many seem reluctant to make this investment today.

Is childhood under attack? Is free play at risk? Is the social contract between adults and children being violated? Some social critics tell us that children are being "hurried,"[19] that children are growing up "without childhood,"[20] and that there is occurring an "erosion of childhood."[21] This suggests that a growing number of American families feel they cannot afford the luxury of childhood and its substantial financial and psychological investment.

How would we know if the protected space that is childhood is being compromised? To answer that question, we need to take a look at the forces that erode, sustain, or enlarge childhood. Childhood changes with changes in society, in the behavior of parents, and in the willingness of the culture to provide opportunities for children to enhance their development. To take our look, we need a perspective.

A Perspective on Childrearing

A sculptor was asked to explain his technique. He struggled for words until the interviewer put her question this way. "Suppose I gave you a block of stone and asked you to carve for me an elephant. How would you proceed?" "Ah," he said, his eyes lighting up. "I would take in hand my chisel and hammer and chip away everything that did not look like an elephant."

He had a perspective. He knew where he was going without being able to specify each movement in advance. The perspective, the vision of the outcome, informed each action and guided each decision.

My principal goal in writing this book is to offer a perspective on childrearing in the 1990s that will illuminate what is happening to our children today and point toward helpful responses we can make as citizens, as professionals, as community leaders, and as parents. This perspective will help us see connections between seemingly unrelated events and information. Armed with this perspective, we can recognize what is going on around us and take steps to make things better. At the heart of my analysis is my belief that when all the data are collected and organized, they present a picture of a much more socially toxic environment for kids in the 90s than for their predecessors in the 50s—or the 60s or 70s for that matter. They also show a greater vulnerability to that social toxicity on the part of today's children due to the buildup of risk factors in their families.

I am certainly not going to suggest that we could solve all our problems by trying to restore the past. We do not want to return to the sexism, racism, or any other form of the discrimination that was so blatant in earlier decades. At the same time, comparing the present to the past can help us identify the risk factors that we must confront if our children are to have the childhoods they need.

This isn't to say that everything for children is worse now than it was in earlier decades, and certainly not that things were perfect then. It is easy to drown in a sea of nostalgia. Some things have gotten better. For example, recent decades have seen important improvements in medical care that have removed many threats to the well-being of children. Polio is but one example—the advent of a vaccination to prevent polio was a cause for widespread celebration. (Having been one of the early "guinea pigs" in the testing of that vaccine, I remember this clearly.) Similarly, childhood cancer was once a nearly automatic death sentence, whereas now most of those affected survive.

By the same token, the decades since the 1950s have seen marked improvement in the decline of "isms" that constricted the development of positive personal and group identity and the full potential of millions. I refer to sexism that limited the choices of girls and women, and imposed many costly adaptations. As but one example, when girls of that era were asked what they wanted to be when they grew up, 90 percent of them answered "mother," "teacher," or "nurse." Boys of the same generation gave answers scattered across a wide range of possibilities, from cowboy to brain surgeon.[22]

And I refer to racism, that into the 1950s (and beyond) made a mockery of concepts like "due process" and "all men are created equal." Blatant racism was uprooted by the civil rights movement, and that is cause for celebration. What's more, other forms of blatant discrimination have receded since the 1950s—in the definition and treatment of the disabled, in the tolerance for dissent, in the humanization of many hitherto maligned categories of persons. All this represents cultural progress, and I salute and appreciate all of it.

Growing egalitarianism within two-parent families, indeed between men and women generally, is a wonderful social change. And, based upon existing research, we can expect it to lead to lower rates of domestic violence among those families fortunate enough to enjoy it. National survey research demonstrated a 50 percent decline in reported child abuse in well-functioning two-parent families from 1975 to 1985.[23] Some of this change seems tied to the greater willingness and ability of women to terminate marriages to violent men. We can applaud the changed roles and rules for women that will reduce the risk of another generation of girls growing up under the dark shadow of sexism. As the father of a daughter, I certainly applaud those changes. However, these positive changes are not the whole story.

For each positive trend there is a downside. Despite the improvements in medicine that have improved the prognosis for childhood cancer victims, the overall rates of cancer have been rising because of the increased physical toxicity of the environment— doubling breast cancer for women and testicular cancer for men, for example. And despite improved technologies for preventing childhood diseases, vaccination rates for children have been dropping in recent years. Many diseases are held at bay, but overall physical condition among children has declined and obesity has increased.

The decline in pernicious "isms" has been paralleled by the rise of fundamentalist ideologies that seek to reinstate oppressive and dehumanizing practices such as "gay bashing." At the same time, fewer and fewer teenagers see that marriage and childrearing go together. A national survey reports that between 1980 and 1991, the percentage of teenagers who believe that it is OK for a man and woman to have and raise a child out of wedlock has increased from 26 percent to 42 percent. Thus, we see both an increase in rigid fundamentalism and a decrease in more basic commitment to traditional family forms.

And while blatant institutionalized racism has declined, inequalities based upon race have if anything increased, and many among disparaged minorities feel increasingly left behind. We remain a segregated society, and racism flourishes. For example, minorities are still subject to discrimination in housing and the granting of credit, and they are often excluded from political power. What is more, social relations remain mired in racism, as the debate over the O. J. Simpson trial in 1995 revealed.

Finally, while the civil rights and vocational aspirations of girls and women have been recognized in the law, the overall position of women as parents is, if anything, worse than it was in the 1950s. Even those fortunate enough to be part of stable two-parent families generally have full-time jobs as well, in addition to bearing the bulk of the responsibility for cooking, cleaning, and child care at home. And more and more women are single parents, either unmarried at the birth of their children or later divorced or abandoned by the children's fathers. What is more, most women are in relatively low-paying jobs, and this means a mother on her own is probably heading up a poor or nearly poor family.

I can acknowledge and celebrate progress in some aspects of American life and yet still maintain that the concept of social toxicity explains a great deal of what troubles us about children and youth growing up in the 1990s. Violence, television, fractured families, big schools, all these topics come into new focus as elements in a larger concept, social toxicity. At stake is the essence of childhood as a protected time and place in the human life cycle. Threats to childhood itself play a central role in the story of growing up in a socially toxic environment.

What Can We Do?

My effort to analyze social toxicity and the ways parents and teachers deal with it must not be understood as an attack on either parents or teachers—I have not fallen prey to the common tendency to blame the victim. Imagine living in a city plagued by cholera. In this city, the challenge to parents to keep kids healthy would be overwhelming. Yes, the most competent parents and those with the most resources would have more success delivering drinkable water to their children than would other parents. But even these effective parents would sometimes fail. Rather than blaming parents for their failure, a reasonable observer would point the finger at the community's failed water purification system. In a socially toxic environment, the same principle holds. We need to put aside blaming parents and take a good hard look at the challenge of raising children in a socially toxic environment.

Chapter Two

Drawing Our Children's Social Maps

When we Americans seek to understand our children, we move most easily among psychological theories that focus on individual development. Our deeply rooted individualistic culture means we are most comfortable approaching our children as individual thinkers (through theories of cognition) or as the sum total of reinforced patterns of behavior (through theories of learning). These approaches tell us a great deal about some specifics of behavior and development. If our goal is to evaluate the quality of our children's lives, however, we need a more avowedly social definition of development, a definition that focuses on the child's relationships.

Children and Childhood

Child development involves many processes and outcomes—the maturation of language, the coordination of mind and body, and the emergence of identity, among others. But first and foremost, child development is about the process and outcome of drawing the child's social map, a map brought to life in behavior as it arises and is understood by the individual and the community. Life draws the child's map; each child sees the world through the lenses of culture, temperament, and individual experience. The child proceeds with the drawing of this map in response to experiences that arise from the social systems of family, school, neighborhood, church, community, society, and culture.

Some children learn to draw social maps in which they are central figures, powerful and surrounded by allies. Others draw defensive maps in which they are surrounded by enemies, or are insignificant specks stuck off in the corner. Does the child expect help when in need? Does the child fear strangers? Does the child trust other children? Does the child expect adults to cause pain? To give comfort? Does the child see a safe and secure place in the world? The social map holds the answers to these questions.

The child's social map is first primarily the result of experience, but increasingly it becomes the cause. I recall a troubled teenager who said in an interview, "When I meet someone new I always do something bad so that I know where I stand." As you might expect, her obnoxious and provocative behavior usually elicited hostility from the adults she met, thus confirming what her internalized map told her, namely that people were bad. "See," she would say, "I told you so." Social maps are like that. They are often self-sustaining. They gather momentum, for better or for worse.

Where Do Social Maps Come From?

Social maps come from the way the child gets along in the world. Our task is to understand the forces of the social environment as they impinge upon the child. One of the first things we can observe in this process is that by and large people become what their environment defines as real and normal. Kids growing up in China become Chinese children. Kids growing up in Nicaragua become Nicaraguan. Kids learn to speak the language they hear around them. They learn the games played by other kids in their community. They become aggressive in violent societies. They learn to read at the "normal" time for their society. Environment guides most of the people most of the time.

Environmental Press

Environmental press is a term used by ecological psychologists to talk about this process of normalization. It includes the combined influence of forces working in a setting to shape the behavior and development of people who are in that setting. Environmental press arises from the circumstances confronting and surrounding an individual. These forces generate psychosocial momentum that guides individuals in a particular direction. It is raw material for children's social maps.

Two investigators who have studied environmental press put it this way: "behavior settings are coercive of behavior. People who enter settings are pressed to help enact its program (while at the same time using the setting for their own purposes)."[1] As time goes on, individual behavior tends to become compatible with the demands of the environment. Thus social maps parallel experience. Some behavior is demonstrated (modeled) and encouraged (reinforced), so it occurs often, while other behavior is rare. It depends on what the environment demands, punishes, or tolerates. People tend to come to resemble the environments they inhabit. Psychologist Rudolph Moos called this the "principle of progressive conformity."[2]

Environmental press arises as the result of all forces at work within an environment. Physical features, for instance, may promote or impede access to desired destinations or alternate uses of existing space. A busy highway may block children from playing in or across the street. Social patterns may encourage one action or discourage another, or reward one value or attitude and punish another. In North America we say, "It's the squeaky wheel that gets the grease," whereas in Japan they say, "It's the nail that sticks out that gets hammered down." Further, these influences interact with and modify each other, so that physical attributes affect social variables and vice versa. Families with more than one television are more likely to end up watching less together as a family. Families with members who find each other's company unpleasant may be inclined to buy several TVs so as to avoid conflict.

Environmental press is at work everywhere. For example, small social environments (towns, groups, institutions) generate patterns of behavior different from large ones. Large settings tend to discourage participation and pro-social behavior while small environments tend to encourage both.[3] Thus, living in a small town is likely to produce a different social map than living in a big city, one that builds in an expectation of neighborliness rather than defensiveness.

Environments in which busy streets separate the places where children live from the places where they can play tend to put children in jeopardy, and thus put pressure on parents to provide regulation.[4] All this can affect the quality and quantity of play, and the whole experience of childhood as a result. Of particular concern are forces that restrict exploration by children. For example, many parents and children today feel intensely the dangers of kidnapping. Listening to some parents talk about this, I believe they have gone beyond concern to outright paranoia. The mass media feed their fear, and this magnifies the threat beyond reasonable size. As a result, children are more and more being denied free run of their neighborhoods and communities in the belief that such freedom would increase their exposure to predatory adults. Their social maps are distorted as a result.

Individual Response

Each individual brings to any situation a unique arrangement of personal resources, a particular level of development, and a current social map. Therefore, different people may react differently to the same environment. Some people are more affected by big environments than others, for example. And the most likely to be affected are the ones who are made vulnerable by their personal history and the balance of strengths and threats in their lives. Here it is again, individual vulnerability to environmental forces.

Furthermore, the same environment may mean something quite different to the same child as time passes. For example, the busy street that was life-threatening to a child of four may be a developmentally appropriate challenge for a nine-year-old, and a mild inconvenience for a teenager. The same gory movie that will prove traumatic for a six-year-old may be only titillating for a thirteen-year-old.

In all environments as in all individuals, there are weaknesses and strengths, sources of risk and opportunity. These forces may work for or against meeting the child's basic survival needs; for or against providing emotional nurturance and continuity; for or against appropriate attempts at self-determination. In short, the nature of the social environment may work for or against the creation of a positive environment for the growth and development of children and their social maps.

Families

One thing that we can establish is the central role of families in the child's experience. The family is the exclusive early environment for most children and the primary environment for nearly all. As such, it is a major source of environmental press. Tell me something about a child's family, and chances are I can tell you something about that child. Will the child do well in school? go to college? become a violent criminal? be poor? become a teenage parent? Family plays a decisive role in answering each of these questions. We know also that children function not so much as individuals but as members of families when it comes to entering and experiencing new environments such as schools. What is more, systems analysis teaches that families themselves develop as they pass through stages in their life course.[5]

As if this were not enough complexity, we must also chart the evolving scope of the child's world as more and more settings are added. The newborn shapes the feeding behavior of its mother, but is confined largely to a crib or a lap, and has limited means of communicating its needs and wants. The ten-year-old, on the other hand, influences many adults and other children located in many different settings, and has many ways of communicating. The world of adolescents is still larger and more diverse, as is their ability to influence it.

At first, most children experience only one social system—the home. Home involves interaction with a very small group of people—often one person at a time—in relatively simple activities such as feeding, bathing, and cuddling that offer the baby an introductory lesson in love. As the child develops, complexity increases; the child does more, with more people, in more places. Play assumes an ever-larger role, and eventually is joined by work.

Playing, working, and loving—the essence of normal human existence—are the principal activities that characterize the child's family in the early years. However, the extent to which these activities take place, their quality, and their level of complexity are variables. This is one way to specify the meaning of childhood itself. How is a healthy balance of playing, working, and loving struck by and for the child?

Cause and Effect

The child and the environment negotiate their relationship as time goes on. Neither is constant; each depends on the other. Does X cause Y? It depends. One cannot predict the future of either X or Y without knowing something about the other. Does a disabled child stand a greater risk of being abused? It depends. Some environments are vulnerable to the stresses of caring for such a child, while others are not. Does economic deprivation harm development? It depends on how old one is when it hits, what sex one is, what the future brings in the way of vocational opportunity, what the quality of family life was in the past, what one's economic expectations and assumptions are, and whether one looks at the short term or the long run.[6]

Clinical psychologists and psychiatrists live with the ambiguity of "it depends" all the time. They know that sometimes a child's behavior means one thing and sometimes another. They know that the impact of a childhood experience depends upon who the child is and what else is happening in the child's life. One child responds to parental pressure as a growth-inducing challenge. Another buckles under the same pressure. My son at age twelve relished Steven King's horror novels; my daughter at the same age was spooked by them. Clinicians know they must deal with all this, but researchers and educators often have a hard time incorporating it into their academic models. They are usually looking for general principles, comprehensive approaches, complete and unambiguous answers.

Urie Bronfenbrenner is one who has accepted the reality of complexity. He sees the child's environment as "a set of nested structures, each inside the next, like a set of Russian dolls."[7] These nested systems mean that if we see children and their parents in conflict over how to spend time together, we need to look outward to the economy that creates economic demands and opportunities, and to the culture that defines a person's personal worth in monetary terms and thus causes parents to consider the costs of time spent on family relations. In addition, we must look inward to the parent-child relationships that are affected by the changing roles and status of the parents and to temperamental characteristics of the individuals involved.

Further, we must look "across" to see how systems beyond the family adjust to changing conditions. For example, what happens if economic pressures increase the need for child care? Schools may respond by extending their institutional coverage to younger (formerly "preschool") children. The net result may be to displace parent-child time together, as younger and younger children are in the system. And, if that system is set up for older children, it may be unresponsive to the special needs of the very young. Narrowly academic activities may take the place of a more developmentally appropriate focus on play unless the curriculum changes.

I vividly recall overhearing a couple of elementary school principals discussing a new state-funded program for four-year-olds in their schools. One of the principals remarked that he had been down to visit the new program in his school, "but all they do is play and eat!" But this is changing in a growing number of developmentally appropriate school-based early childhood programs under the leadership of groups like "The School of the 21st Century" (founded by Edward Zigler at Yale University) and the National Association for the Education of Young Children. More schools are providing good developmental homes for young children.

The Ecology of Childhood

Where do we look to find influences on the quality of the child's life, the richness of the child's social map, and the degree to which childhood is fostered and protected? Influential events often occur in systems where children do not themselves participate directly. In these remote environments, things happen that have a direct impact on parents and other adults who interact with children. Indeed, such influences are one of the driving forces behind increased social toxicity for children.

For example, when parents work in settings that demand conformity rather than self-direction, they reflect this orientation in their childrearing, tending to stifle independence and emphasize obedience.[8] Other influential elements of the work environment include long or inflexible hours, commuting, business travel, or job-related stress that impoverishes family life.

But this is not all. When the school board mandates early schooling that supplants free play with narrow academic curricula, they undermine childhood. When the planning commission runs a highway through traditional free play areas, it jeopardizes child development. When parents are under pressure from their peers to involve very young children in formal activities, opportunities for free play may diminish. When parents are forced to place their children in substandard child care because the community does not make sure that good care is available, the ensuing risk may impair development.

The status of childhood and children is often a political matter, a matter of who has the power to shape the institutional life of the community, and how they use that power. For example, Roderick Wallace has demonstrated how politically motivated decisions to close firehouses and reduce the number of firefighters in New York City in the late 1970s led to a significant increase in large fires. These fires destroyed the physical environment and set in motion an eventual decline in the quality of the social environment for poor children.[9]

This is how the ecological pieces fit together. They reflect a cultural blueprint of what is normal, what is obvious, and what is impossible. These blueprints reflect a people's shared assumptions about how things should be done, about the norms for understanding how development proceeds. They define childhood.

The blueprints of childhood can include a national economic policy that tolerates poverty and increases the chances of economic dislocation for families with young children. Or the blueprints can include a national economic policy that insists upon an economic floor for all families. They can include high levels of geographic mobility that disrupt neighborhood and school connections and the social network of parents, or they can support stability. They can script a neglect of parents' needs in favor of the needs of corporations for mobile workers. Or they can include an active effort to support parents as workers. They can include patterns of racist or sexist values that demean and shame large numbers of parents, thereby undermining the psychological security of their children and threatening each child's self-esteem. Or they can include messages of affirmation and acceptance.

While the family is usually the most important social system for a young child, the overall impact of the environment emerges from the balance among all these influences—culture, economies, politics, biology, and the psychological ebb and flow of day-to-day life. One astute observer puts it this way:

The nature of a society at a given time shapes the structure of social classes; social class influences the nature of family life and experience; racial membership influences likely occupation; through income, occupation helps determine neighborhood. Neighborhood determines where one goes to school, and not only is family background associated with how a child does in school, but it may influence how the school treats a child and the ability of the child and family to manipulate the institutional ropes of a school . . . and so on in a series of permutations, combinations, and feedback loops. In the midst of this complex, breathing organism called social structure is the child.[10]

This is what childhood is all about. Offering the young human organism a special opportunity to play and to love and be loved and to learn to be competent so that the child may reach for the fullness of human development. Childhood is about learning the ropes of the family, the community, and the culture, all in child-sized doses, on a child's timetable, in ways that enhance the child's eventual successful transition to adulthood. We have learned that the process of development arises through the learning of useful and affirming social maps of the world. It is not simply a realization of the child's internal agenda—although that biological agenda plays an important role. It is not simply the functioning of the family as a social system—although this too is vitally important.

In fact, development results from a complex interplay among these child and family systems and the social environment within which both children and families operate. And this is the reason why I find myself so deeply disturbed about what seems to be happening in that social environment, and happening at a time in the social history of families when more and more children are more and more vulnerable to negative influences in the social environment because of family disruptions linked to divorce, separation, and abandonment.

Television as a Feature of
the Socially Toxic Environment

Searching for the origins and consequences of social toxicity, I find myself drawn to the significance of television in the culture of childhood and family life. Mine is the last generation of Americans who will have any memory of life BTV—before television. It was in 1936 that British social psychologist T. H. Pear asked, "What differences will television make to our habits and mental attitudes?" Sixty years later, we are beginning to find out.

Television has succeeded beyond its early proponents' wildest dreams in becoming the dominant cultural force in our society. Survey research reports that only a minority of Americans read a whole book in any given year. In contrast, virtually everyone reports watching television. Indeed, the television we watch has become the binding force in our culture, perhaps one of the few common elements. But what exactly is common to that experience?

I think the best metaphor for understanding the consequences of television on childhood and youth is to be found in the effects of dietary fat on health. For instance, while some fat is essential to a tasty and healthy diet, quantity and quality matter. Too much fat becomes a problem, especially too much saturated fat. Most Americans consume well beyond the recommended daily requirement of sixty grams. As a result, we are vulnerable to heart disease and obesity.

So it is with television consumption, I think. In small doses, and of the right type, television can be healthy. It can entertain. It can even teach. It becomes a problem, though, in that Americans watch too much of it, and too much of the wrong kind.

It's important to realize that we have a hard time studying the effects of television because it is so deeply embedded in today's society and culture. Who can be an appropriate comparison group for studying the effects of television? Those few who don't watch are such an unrepresentative group that we would be hard pressed to draw general conclusions from studying them. Ask a fish to describe water; ask an American to analyze television—it is almost as universal a fact of life. And yet, television contributes to the social toxicity of the environment for children and families, who survive in much the same fashion as fish surviving in polluted water, growing twisted and strange. I base this conclusion on two sources: historical research and my reading of contemporary studies.

Drawing upon these sources, I see the consequences of television viewing in two principal ways. The first is its role in transmitting and validating messages about violence and aggression in human interactions. The hundreds and hundreds of existing studies leave little doubt on this. Like a steady diet of saturated fat, the violence that saturates television becomes bad for your health (and mine too, if I'm the target of your aggression). One recent analysis concludes that the introduction of television resulted in a doubling of the homicide rate.[11] Other studies document a doubling of aggressive behavior among children after television was introduced into their community.[12]

As television violence increased through the 1960s and 1970s, it was doing so in a changed social context, a context in which declining adult presence in the lives of children was setting those children up to take in the messages of violence with less and less counter socialization from adults. TV thus plays a role *both* in increasing the level of social toxicity and in increasing the vulnerability of children to that toxicity. These two features of social toxicity—violent messages and decreased adult influence—work together in a conspiratorial fashion.

And today, we reap the bitter fruits of that development: arrests of juveniles for violent crime increased from a rate of 137 per 100,000 in 1965 to 437 per 100,000 in 1990; teen suicides went from 3.6 per 100,000 in 1955 to 11.3 per 100,000 in 1990.[13] A recent review of the existing research by the American Psychological Association concluded that television is responsible for up to

15 percent of the violent behavior of America's children and youth.[14] That figure is probably an underestimate, however, because it is based upon studies of the violent content of TV, and does not include the effects of reduced child-adult interaction in the home and the community.

Besides teaching that violence is an acceptable means of conflict resolution, television has another and more insidious effect on human development. By crowding out activities that used to be shared with family and friends, thus substituting passive observation for real social interaction, television deprives people of vital lessons in living together. The less experience people have with face-to-face interaction, the more they distrust each other, the more hostile and defensive their social maps become, and the more toxic the social environment becomes. I'll return to this topic in Chapter Five and Chapter Seven. However, in addition to the behavioral problems and lost experience associated with excessive television exposure, there is still another problem—the simple nastiness of much of the programming combines with other factors in the environment to undercut the development of a strong and positive mental map of a child's world.

Nastiness

While the number of children who have experienced violence personally is still limited, all of our children are now being exposed regularly to nastiness. Its effects may be less dramatic, but nastiness does also harm our children. The nastiness they see and hear interferes with their happiness and the future they see for themselves, and thus represents a pervasive threat to children at every level of society in every community.

Childhood ought to be a protected space for children in the economic, political, and sexual life of the community. When we allow the erosion of this protected cultural space for childhood, we permit the creation of one important element of social toxicity—

and it happens daily. It is, some observers say, like "the end of child-hood" when children are exposed to and drawn into adult issues and themes well before their time.

There are many signs that this is happening. For example, many children faithfully follow TV soap operas, listen to raunchy pop music, and speak in the clichés of adulthood. Like many features of increased social toxicity, this erosion of childhood is hard to detect most of the time because it is so widespread. I notice it most when I happen upon a child who somehow has been spared, who vividly reminds me of what childhood was before. These children are polite. They are interested in the culture of childhood—toys and games, and books that are not preoccupied with sexual violence. Meeting such a child is a bit like looking at a family photo album from the 1950s.

Children today are certainly aware of adult issues like rape, mur-der, infidelity, and all the other nastiness that adults must at least acknowledge. I consider this to be part of the problem of social tox-icity because children are not well prepared to deal with these issues. Children are not simply short adults. Their thinking and feel-ing are different—in many ways more concrete, personalized, and limited.

Children lack the social resources and personal power to deal with adult issues. Of course, even many adults sometimes feel over-whelmed when faced with the problems of the world—war, poverty, injustice, domestic violence, environmental degradation, commu-nity catastrophe. I recognize that all too well, having devoted a major part of my professional life to working with child abuse, fam-ily poverty, and children in war zones.

But children face a special challenge in dealing with these issues because of their relative powerlessness. Indeed, one line of psycho-logical theorizing has gone so far as to identify powerlessness as the primary factor leading to impaired development and psycho-pathology.[15] The ancient Greek philosopher Herodotus recognized this when he said, "There is no greater sorrow in life than to have an understanding of many things but power over nothing." This is the situation many children face in our society. They are aware but powerless. No wonder there is more childhood depression and sadness than before. No wonder so many children seem so world-weary at such a young age—they have had to stretch their maps of the world to include so many things they cannot hope to deal with.

I thought of this one day when I was visiting a third-grade classroom in a middle-class suburban elementary school. In the course of my discussion with the children, they talked about the recent kidnappings of children that had been in the news, of the docudrama "reality" programs on television like *Cops* and *Rescue 911* that frightened them, of the soap operas, MTV, and violent movies they watched, of the many experiences of divorce and separation in their lives, of the fact that a third of them went home to empty houses after school every day.

And then I asked them to close their eyes and tell me what words, thoughts, and feelings came to them when I said "*Mr. Rogers*." I could see the smiles on their faces, the faces of children remembering something very positive, the soft features of the young at heart. "Kind." "Gentle." "Cares about you." "King Friday." "The Trolley." "Nice," they said. I had touched something with which they had myriad positive associations.

Then I asked them to close their eyes again and tell me what they thought of when I said "*Beavis and Butthead.*" (This is a popular cable television cartoon aimed at teenagers that features a couple of low and nasty guys, and virtually all the kids said they had watched it.) Now the associations were of a very different character. "Nasty." "Mean." "Fires." "Rude." "Hurting people." "Bad," they said without hesitation. Even their little faces were scrunched up and harder looking. When we talked about it later, they said that Mr. Rogers was history for them. "He was from our childhood; Beavis and Butthead are today," said one of the children, all of eight years old. *Mr. Rogers* is history for them; *Beavis and Butthead* is the present. Witness the end of childhood.

This experience crystallized for me the nastiness to which children are exposed so early in life. *Beavis and Butthead* is part of it. But there's more: the constant exposure to stories of missing children, kidnapped children, abused children, and murdered children. A study conducted in Ohio with elementary-school-aged kids reported that 43 percent of the fourth through sixth graders thought it was "likely" that they would be kidnapped at some point in their lives.[16]

Does anyone doubt that today's children are more wary of strangers than they were a generation ago, that on a day-to-day basis they feel less safe? Among teenagers we find evidence of growing paranoia. In 1975, 35 percent of high school seniors surveyed believed "most people can be trusted." By 1992, that figure had decreased to 19 percent. Correspondingly, in 1975, 40 percent of the teenagers surveyed said "you can't be too careful in dealing with people." By 1992, that figure was 60 percent.[17]

But it is more than extreme evils that concern me here. It is the low-grade nastiness that surrounds and increasingly infuses all our children and threatens to overwhelm their future with cynicism. I disliked the movie *Home Alone* in part because it glorified this nastiness (not to mention the film's graphic violence). I hear more and more kids using what we used to call "foul language," and using it in a casual way. I think it coarsens them; it affects the way they value (or devalue) everything around them. It adds to the nastiness, and bodes ill for our future as a society.

A first-grade teacher told me recently that last Halloween some of the boys in her class came to school dressed up as Freddy Krueger and other horrific characters from popular slasher movies. One of them explained to the class that he was Jack the Ripper. "Do you know who he was?" he asked the other six-year-olds. "He raped and killed women," he explained with a leer. "Cool," responded the other boys. Indeed.

The decline in civility (an old-fashioned word to be sure) is more than shocking. It has a negative effect on our children's development. It lowers the level of discourse. It provokes a callousness that generalizes to other relationships. It erodes the special place in the life of our culture we used to call childhood.

Most people now recognize that psychological maltreatment is a real threat to healthy development. I believe that children are living with more psychological maltreatment now. Psychological maltreatment includes rejecting, terrorizing, and corrupting.[18] Today's children experience a great deal of rejection. For example, when their fathers disappear from their lives after separation and divorce, many children feel rejected. More than half of divorced fathers have little or no contact with their children, and even the most connected are at least partially absent due to custody arrangements. Children also feel rejected when parents cannot find time for them. As to terror, today's young children are likely to be exposed to traumatic terror at the movies or at home watching the TV, even if they're fortunate enough to avoid the real thing. And corrupting? It seems self-evident that today's children are being corrupted by the nastiness that surrounds them. They are sexualized by the sexuality that pervades the imagery on television and the movies. They are desensitized to aggression by the ceaseless violence that washes over them.

A survey commissioned by the National Committee to Prevent Child Abuse in 1985 asked adults, "How likely do you think it is that repeated yelling and swearing at a child leads to long term emotional problems for the child?" Three-quarters of the respondents said they thought it was "likely" or "very likely," and I agree. That's one reason why I worry about the nastiness of rhetoric in families, in schools, and on the streets. Nastiness corrodes our children's social maps; it is the last thing children need, especially here and now when they face so many other challenges.

What Can We Do?

Knowing that social map making is one of the most important developmental tasks of childhood, we must pay more attention to what children are seeing, hearing, and feeling about the world. Children are like sponges; they soak up what is around them and then release it when squeezed. We must work together as parents, citizens, and professionals to protect childhood, and thus children. Be cautious and conservative about exposing children to the nastiness of the world. Let them play freely. Let them take childhood at a child's pace. Parents and teachers should be the guardians of childhood and should band together to shield the children in their care from premature adolescence—in clothing, language, television, and social activities. Keep the dark side of adult life within the adult circle as much as possible. Risk accumulates, so we must do all we can to spare children what we can so that they can deal with what we cannot.

Chapter Three

Stability

Making Families Strong

Growing up in the 1950s, I lived in an average family. By the standards of that time, I thought we were middle class, perhaps *lower* middle class, but middle class nonetheless. We had food on the table. We owned a house. We had a car and a television set. We went to the movies from time to time. We went on vacation every few years (usually to visit relatives). But from a modern child's perspective, we appear poor. We didn't go out to eat very often. Our house had only one bathroom. We had only one car and one television set, and we bought new clothes mainly each September at back-to-school sales. I had a paper route, and we played ball in the street.

My children belong to a different world, not just because I make more money than my father did, but because the social environment has changed. The world of my childhood is nearly unfathomable to my kids. They cannot really believe what my life was like as a kid growing up in the 1950s in the New York metropolitan area. They have difficulty understanding the nostalgic pride with which I talk about the relative simplicity of those times. TV entered our lives, but with only a handful of channels and no VCR. When we played on the street it was in canvas sneakers, not leather running shoes. We had board games like Monopoly, but no Nintendo.

When we thought about the world it was in simple, child-sized terms, not with the apparent sophistication of today's kids. The people across the street got furious if you accidentally hit a ball onto their lawn, but no one ever thought of suing anybody over it. The man down the street did some crazy things (like dressing up as the

New Year's Baby on New Year's Eve and then getting in an accident in his car and getting arrested), but we kids didn't know he was an *alcoholic*. It wasn't until I was nineteen that I even realized that my parents had been separated briefly when I was two years old. I had always known that my mother and I had gone to live with her parents for the better part of a year, but no one had defined it as being *separated*.

Sometimes I feel like a dinosaur trying to explain what life was like before mammals when I talk to my children about the old days, they who know about divorce firsthand, they who cannot avoid knowing about rape and murder and the other staples of the daily news, they who know so much about AIDS, drugs, genocide, and sexual abuse.

The kids and I were driving in our car, reenacting a routine many parents know well. My daughter was speaking for the realities of her times. I was trying to explain what was gone and what was missing, whatever benefits may have accrued in the changing times. I suppose I had assumed the instructional mode into which we parents often sink. Finally my daughter put this all to rout: "Dad," she said with a rhetorical flourish, "it ain't the 50s anymore."

It Ain't the 50s Anymore . . . or the 60s . . . or the 70s

Kahlil Gibran's poem "On Children" includes these words: "For their souls dwell in the house of tomorrow, which you cannot visit, not even in your dreams."[1] Gibran was fashionable in the 1960s. But I read this line differently now, in the 1990s. I survey the childhood of my children and that of my nephews and niece, and the other children and young parents I meet. I compare it with the childhood I shared with my brother and sister, and I feel strongly that Gibran's analysis misses the point entirely. The point for my children is this: my soul dwells in a place where they cannot go, and I think they and all the other children (and young parents who themselves were born in the 1970s) are the worse for it.

Gibran wrote to parents that their children belong to the future: "They belong to tomorrow where you cannot go." Yet as I get older and my childhood recedes further and further into history, I find myself wanting to tell the children of the 90s quite the opposite message: "Children, your parents (or grandparents) belong to a place where you cannot go. It is called the 1950s."

However, while I cannot go to my children's future, they can at least view my past. They can do this in the reruns of family sitcoms from the 1950s that appear nightly on cable television on Nickelodeon's *Nick at Nite*. They can travel back to *Leave it to Beaver*, *The Donna Reed Show*, *Father Knows Best*, and *The Dick Van Dyke Show*, among others.

And what do they think when they visit these ancient places? My teenage son is pretty clear on this point. To him the TV families of the 50s and early 60s seem "more formal, and a bit more strict." But he adds, this is good. He admires the "stability" of these families and their "kindness"—in contrast to the "out of control" families he knows—"divorced families" as he calls them.

My daughter seems to share his view. The TV families seem almost "too perfect" to her, but she too finds the message of stability and "niceness" reassuring. When I ask her about the world the TV families inhabit, my question is this: does it seem safe? She nods her head vigorously, "Yes!" In a way, these two time travelers sum up much of what the 1950s represent: "formal but nice, structured but safe."

Other children, interviewed by *Chicago Tribune* journalist Jennifer Mangan, reflect more clearly the damage that the intervening decades have wrought on families and thus on children and childhood.[2] Says one thirteen-year-old girl, "Those kids are not normal. If those were my kids, I would send them to get psychiatric help." I'm shocked, because she is speaking of Wally and Beaver Cleaver—not Beavis and Butthead. And a thirteen-year-old boy adds, "It's so much different now. The kids in the old shows get in trouble for sticking out their tongue. Today, kids on TV are crashing cars, stealing money from their parents, and degrading them." Adds a sixteen-year-old girl, speaking of the current family sitcoms, "They talk back all the time and are always fighting. Times were better back then; the conflicts and problems weren't as serious as today."

The two recent family sitcoms that do seem to capture the spirit of the old shows for children are *Wonder Years*, which is about a child of the 1950s who is facing adolescence in the 1960s, and *The Cosby Show*, which offers a similar throwback to innocence even though the setting is contemporary. *Cosby* manages to retain the safety, stability, and civility of the earlier era while updating the husband-wife dynamic somewhat and making the wife a career woman. As many observers have noted, the show is best understood as an African-American *Father Knows Best*. And what is *Father Knows Best?* It is the ideal of two-parent, middle-class family life: two loving and steady parents who make a home for their children and meet their obligations to be good citizens and reliable workers.

I think many kids long for the kind of families portrayed on *Nick at Nite*. They long for the stability, the safety, the fact that the parents are adults and the kids are children. Of course, most children are unaware of what it costs many adults to stay in unsatisfying or conflictual marriages "for the sake of the children." Children are very conservative at heart, responding as they do to regularity, predictability, and stability. A sixth-grade teacher recently asked her students to write essays about their "ideal families." Rachel wrote the following:

"My ideal father would be nice, caring, he would listen to what you say and would *not* embarrass you in public (that means he won't turn me upside down in public). He would work till five and play games instead of sit in his room and read his newspaper. My ideal mother would be nice, very caring. She would listen to you and not comment, and try to understand your feelings instead of saying, 'Think about me.' She would come home at three."[3]

Mr. Cleaver and Donna Reed are alive and well in the hearts of young children. What kids want is Mom and Dad, not some cool friend. Part of our challenge today is to see what we can do about offering children family experiences that meet this conservative need and yet recognize the realities of adult life: today's marriages are based on higher expectations on the part of women (and men) for equality, dignity, independence, and a sense of fulfillment. Divorce is a fact of life for many of us, as men and women seek to make the best of their lives as individuals, and family relationships must be undertaken to reflect that reality and still do a good job of meeting the needs of children.

Beyond Nostalgia

The 1950s. It seems like ancient history to many of today's parents, who were born in the 1960s and 1970s. But there are some important lessons to be learned from families in the 1950s. Beyond the simple nostalgia that many people of my age feel, and the disdain of many younger people, there is some core of truth to the belief that the 1950s offered something distinctly attractive to children and to those who care about children. That something is family stability.

The 1950s were an oasis of stability for the family in America. After decades, even centuries of family instability due to premature death and desertion linked to economic crisis, the 1950s provided something very different. More people married. They married earlier and more permanently. They had more children and had children earlier. They were more likely to live in intact two-parent families than did people before or after that time.

Prior to World War II, many young families had to live under the thumb of older relatives or had to house those relatives, more out of obligation and grim economic necessity than out of generosity of spirit. The affluence of the 1950s permitted more family independence. Recall also that in the decades before World War II it was much more common for families to be split apart because of premature death of a parent or because fathers left to seek relief from economic pressures. The 1950s changed that dramatically.

Remember too that in the early decades of this century it was common for families to include nonparental adults, often boarders taken in because families needed the income. According to one estimate, about a third of family households contained an unrelated adult.

Thus, the 1950s represent a special period in the history of the American family. In the decades that came after, all the trends that had been evident before World War II picked up steam and overcame the reversals of the 50s. Demographer Andrew Cherlin has chronicled this story well.[4] The divorce rate rose dramatically. It doubled from the 50s to the 60s, and doubled again by the 80s, only now leveling off in the 90s. In 1960, nearly 80 percent of all children were living with both biological parents. By 1990, only about 50 percent were. Now, about half of all marriages end in divorce, and about half of all children spend some or all of their first eighteen years in a single-parent household (either due to divorce or to having been born to single parents). In 1960, about 5 percent of all births were to single mothers. In 1990, it was more than 25 percent.

Despite their growing numbers, U.S. society is not set up well for single-parent families. Economically and socially, these families have much more difficulty achieving and maintaining the independence that is an assumption upon which our policies and practices are based. In our society at present, single-parent families are less able to take care of themselves than two-parent families. If we could address *that* problem through more supportive economic and social arrangements, we could do much to ensure that single-parent families could do a better job of addressing the basic need for stability that children bring with them into the world.

The economic penalty of single parenthood is an urgent problem in its own right. Women still make on average only 70 percent of what men earn—up from 60 percent a generation ago, but often not enough for a family. Many absent fathers do not provide child support. Communities are not set up to meet the child care needs of single mothers. One recent analysis found that much of the negative effect on children associated with divorce is actually the result of the economic decline that mothers and children suffer as a result of divorce.[5] Poverty is an enemy of family stability. I'll return to this point in Chapter Eight, but for now let's return to the matter of being a parent in today's environment.

What's Parenting All About?

For the past twenty-five years I have been talking about children and families with professionals and parents in towns and cities all over the United States and around the world. I have also been conducting research and reading other people's research in an effort to figure out what to tell the people who come searching for answers.

My observations of children and child development over the last twenty-five years persuade me that raising children is anything but simply following directions. As I said in Chapter Two, when the question is, Does X cause Y?, the answer is, It depends. In my travels around the world—six continents, twenty countries—and in my research closer to home, I am struck by the complexity of the task, not the simplicity. We won't make progress in detoxifying the social environment and strengthening children to resist what we can't prevent if we don't acknowledge that complexity.

What I generally find unsatisfying in advice books about child-rearing is the tendency to oversimplify. Many times parents are offered recipes, as if raising a child were like baking a cake—a simple and predictable matter of following directions. If I have learned anything, it is that child development is anything but simple, particularly today, given the complexity of the world for children and adults alike.

Stable Families and Vulnerability to Risk Factors

The social toxicity of today's environment places extreme demands on parents, demands to raise children who can grow up healthy in a sick environment. The institution of the family is one of the important battlegrounds in any effort to deal with and overcome social toxicity. Strong families can prepare children to handle almost anything, but weak families make children vulnerable to even mild threats from the outside world. At the heart of the matter are loving parents who communicate their love, and who teach children a set of positive values through word and deed, even if they are struggling with adult issues like marital conflict, separation, and divorce. Family strength transcends family structure; it derives from a process, not a formal arrangement.

Generally, it seems the children whose families are in disarray or are in some way dysfunctional are most at risk from factors outside the family. For example, children who face domestic violence are the most vulnerable to the effects of growing up amid community violence.[6] They are the ones who show the most psychological problems and model the aggression they see elsewhere. The experience of violence at home does not make these children immune to the violence outside, it makes them more vulnerable to it.

Stability also matters when it comes to risk factors within children themselves. For example, a study conducted in the 1980s examined the consequences of being born with what the researchers called "a minor physical anomaly," such as a mild nervous system problem, a somewhat distorted facial feature, or a minor physical deformity. Such anomalies were used in this study as indicators that something had gone a bit wrong during pregnancy.[7] At issue was whether starting off on the wrong foot this way predicted later problems with aggression—specifically, being arrested for violent offenses by age twenty-one. The investigators examined this relationship in two groups—those children who grew up in "stable" families (those where economic and social conditions remained adequate) and those who grew up in "unstable" families (those where they did not).

The findings were dramatic. Children who grew up in stable families had about the same rate of being arrested for violent offenses (15 percent) whether or not they had been born with minor physical anomalies. By contrast, the difference was striking among unstable families. Of the children of these families who had no minor physical anomalies, 20 percent had been arrested for a violent offence—an unstable family does make life harder for anyone. However, *70 percent* of the children of these families who were born with minor physical anomalies had been arrested for a violent offense by the time they were twenty-one. This study tells us that family stability matters a great deal when it comes to protecting children from risk factors they carry with them, just as family stability matters in protecting children from falling prey to the cultural poisons that surround them.

This conclusion can't be generalized to every individual, of course. Some children are so loaded with personal risk factors that they cannot cope, even when they come from a strong family. These kids are programmed for trouble. By the same token, some environments are so malicious that even a robust child from a strong family can be overwhelmed; bad things can and do happen to good people. What is more, it is a mistake to believe that the family is the only institution in the society that can resist social toxicity, that the family is the only place where kids can become strong.

Schools, churches, and neighborhoods play a role in many cases, and could play a role in more if we devoted our collective efforts to making sure they operate in a fashion that builds resilience and robustness. Of course, we must not forget that we can clean up the toxicity in the social environment in much the same way that we have made progress in cleaning up the physical environment. After decades of effort, many once-polluted rivers and lakes are now in recovery; we could do the same for our culturally polluted streets and air waves.

Social pollution does parallel physical pollution. If we detoxified television and movies, more children and teenagers would face a less socially toxic environment. Thus, the most vulnerable among them would have a much better chance of making it through adolescence without falling victim to alienation, antisocial behavior, and self-destructive patterns. Reduce social toxicity and we will reduce the pressure on families to prepare their children to resist the poisons. This is particularly important now, when nearly half of America's children are growing up in families facing the extra social, psychological, and economic challenges of raising children in a single-parent household.

But central to any initiative must be efforts to improve the capacity of families to rear children who can resist social toxicity. Our toxic environment will be with us for a long time to come, even if we start now in reducing it. To improve our chances for doing so we must start by understanding the family as a social system, with predictable sources of strength and vulnerability. As social systems, families share some basic operating concepts and principles with physical systems. They need energy and established boundaries, and they seek equilibrium.

All systems run on energy. In the case of families, this energy can arise from many sources—tradition, love, economic necessity. Energy comes from family members' personalities, heritage, skills, and interests. But it also comes from outside the family system, from other systems and individuals in their interaction with the family. As families become less capable of independence, they place greater demands upon other systems for the energy needed to meet their basic objectives, including raising their children. This is one reason why single-parent families, particularly those headed by a single woman not receiving child support from the father of her children, are generally more fragile than two-parent families. Energy is at a premium in such families as they struggle to cover all the childrearing bases. The same is true of two-parent, dual-income families struggling to maintain a middle-class existence. The rat race siphons off energy from children and childrearing.

All systems must create a set of boundaries. These boundaries establish who is inside and who is outside. For families, the setting of boundaries is crucial. But there are dangers associated both with being closed off and being too open; balance is essential. Of perhaps equal importance is the nature of the boundaries, how permeable they are to the flow of information, energy, and people across them. Family systems that become cut off run the risk of becoming depleted. In a society like ours that values independence, depletion is a special risk faced by isolated single-parent families, just as it is for dual-income, two-parent families that are closed to community support. On the other hand, family systems that are too open to the outside world may run the risk of being overwhelmed by the toxic forces at work in that world. Turning off the television, or at least cutting down the time it is in use and monitoring and regulating what children watch, is one way to establish family boundaries to reduce the flow of social toxicity into the lives of children.

Systems seek equilibrium. They never achieve it permanently, of course, but a system that cannot find some way to manage stress and to right itself when pushed over is in deep trouble. Inside the family system boundaries are structures of meaning and relationship that govern how the family works on a day-to-day basis to achieve stability. In adjusting to the forces of change from within and without, the family system develops and implements a set of strategies and rules for adapting and coping. Strong families utilize loving messages and open and clear communication of needs and rights to reestablish equilibrium. Weak families take the route of denying reality to avoid having to deal with it, sacrificing members for the good of the whole, and falsely reinterpreting events to make them seem compatible with family needs. All these ploys seem to make sense at the time, but tend to be quite costly to the psychological well-being of family members.

One justified criticism of family life in the 1950s was that it cost mothers too much. Their sacrifices provided much of the energy needed to keep families going. Betty Friedan's *The Feminine Mystique* exposed this problem once and for all.[8] Today, men and women in families struggle to find alternatives to the family that separated the homemaker and breadwinner roles. Judging from the high level of stress exhibited by many, many parents today, and the large number of marriages that end in divorce, it seems clear we haven't finished adjusting to the feminist critique of 1950s families.

We have changed, but not achieved a new equilibrium, due in large measure to the combination of male intransigence at home (unwillingness to compensate for changed maternal roles by assuming an equal share of the day-to-day household and childrearing tasks) and inflexibility in the workplace (scheduling that adds to maternal stress). But some families succeed, even today when the pressures are so great. It is useful to look at what we know about these successful families.

What Makes a Family Successful?

This question resembles a Rorschach inkblot test: what you see reflects who you are and where you've been. Our definition of family success depends on our personal experiences, our beliefs, our deeply held convictions and our hopes. Some people look at traditional families with a dominant father and everyone else subservient and see success. Others see the same family as a prison for its women and children. Some people look at a modern egalitarian family and see success. Others see such a family as a threat to traditional values. However, as is the case with a Rorschach inkblot, we can move beyond mere opinion to look at research that examines the common elements of families with successful outcomes as measured by competent children, contented adults, and family durability.

Families exist in large part to rear children. Therefore, one measure of the success of a family is its ability to do what it takes to turn infants into competent human beings. How do we measure human competence? Loving, working, and playing well is a good start, as I said before. A successful family produces children who are emotionally robust, who can find a place for themselves in the workplace, and who can form and sustain enduring relationships.

A second element in family success is creating a situation in which adults can live with self-respect and some measure of personal fulfillment. It does no good to talk about successful families in terms of child development if meeting those goals destroys the adults who must bear and care for those children. One achievement of modern feminism has been to illuminate the costs borne by women in traditional families. Once the threat was mainly to the physical well-being of women as mothers, who died or were disabled in large numbers through the medical complications of childbearing. Now the greater threat is that the social and emotional demands of childrearing in the modern family will prove too much for ordinary mortals. If families can only succeed with Super Moms and Super Dads at the helm, then what hope is there for us regular folks? So a successful family also produces contented adults.

A third element of a successful family lies in its ability to maintain its core functions as it adapts to changes in marital arrangements. This is a big issue now. Strong families find ways to cope with the traumatic changes associated with divorce. They learn to emphasize the extended, as opposed to the nuclear, family. This may involve greater reliance on grandparents, aunts, uncles, siblings, and cousins. It may involve greater reliance on professional services such as family therapists, to facilitate psychological adjustment. It may mean more use of community resources such as child care. It may mean working extra hard to retain family traditions and retreats despite marital dissolutions. It may mean blending families together through remarriage and complicated "step" relationships. Above all else, it means striving to sustain a child's sense of being part of a strong *family*, even if the child's parents are not husband and wife. It is difficult, but it can be done.

These three criteria provide some of the background for looking at research on family strengths and weaknesses. This research often takes the form of identifying successful families who are nominated one way or another (by other parents, by schools, by agencies, or by churches) and then studying the attributes of those families. Taking a look at that research, we find some common themes. Each of these themes contains a lesson for those who make social policy or conduct parent education or seek to increase social support in communities. Each has special significance for reducing social toxicity or children's vulnerability to it.

One list of characteristics for strong families includes the following elements:[9]

Appreciation. The members regard each other warmly, positively, and give support to each other as individuals. This is vitally important for both children and adults. A family that appears successful from the outside may not be working well on the inside, in the feelings among its members. Psychological acceptance is a wellspring of self-esteem, and self-esteem feeds competence. Rejection, on the other hand, has the opposite effect, choking off self-esteem and leading to a self-fulfilling prophecy of incompetence.[10] When parents reject each other, their children often feel rejected as well. This happens even though the parents never intended such a side effect and may not realize that it has occurred. This is an important message for divorcing spouses.

Spending time together. Strong families spend time together and enjoy it. Being a family is not a hypothetical exercise. It takes time to knit a family together and to keep it from unraveling. This is a big issue for today's families, what with commuting, TV, dual-earner marriages, divorce, and the like. Eating together, working together on projects, participating together in community and school activities, this is the stuff of which successful families are made. Divorced spouses should remember this as they seek ways to meet their continuing responsibilities as *parents*.

Good communication patterns. Family members are honest, open, and receptive toward each other. The process of seeking to maintain equilibrium within the family system thrives on communication. Families with huge domains of silence become vulnerable to serious disequilibrium. Families can handle a lot of change and stress if they keep talking things through, sharing needs, fears, joys, and strategies for coping. The result is a common social map that helps the whole family know where it is. Even after divorce, one key to the future well-being of children is the ability of parents and children to communicate well.

Commitment. The family unit is important to its members, as are the interpersonal subsystems within the family, so that much energy and time are directed inward toward the family as a unit. Choosing family activities is often difficult, because many tempting but essentially solitary activities lure family members apart. However, particularly today, commitment is an essential element in successful families. All the members need to live their lives with the needs of family high on the agenda, so that the family will maintain the strength needed to help them to get through stressful times and deal with environmental pressures. This may be particularly true for families coping with divorce, where an even higher level of commitment to family is necessary to make things work for kids.

Religious orientation. Caring for the soul is an important function of a strong family. Strong families seem anchored in a sense of purpose—usually religious or spiritual in its foundation, sometimes secular—that provides the strength required for commitment to the family as well as to the larger purpose. A family that merely exists, without working for something outside itself, falls apart easily. Cut off from the well of the soul, members often lose track of the reasons for attending to anything but their own passing preferences. This is one reason why religious institutions must open their arms and hearts to divorcing families, not abandon them when they most need spiritual support.

Ability to deal with crises in a positive manner. Strong families can deal with conflicts, and their members band together in mutual support when bad times arise. Life always has thorns as well as roses. Almost every family faces painful challenges—illness, injury, death, separation and divorce, unemployment, natural disaster, crime. Successful families rally together to meet these challenges, and may even emerge stronger from them. Vulnerable families fall apart or sacrifice members. Even the ultimate family challenge, divorce, need not be overwhelming for a strong family, particularly if the focus is on the extended family and if the separated spouses cooperate on behalf of the children.

There are many lists like this one,[11] but one factor they all have in common is stability. Strong families are *reliable*—"good old Mom and Dad." This consistency is reassuring for children, even today when the simpler family forms of the 1950s are being replaced by the complexity of the 1990s. It's what family is all about from a child's perspective. Stability. But this stability is more than just a matter of family systems. It's also a matter of a place called home.

Home from a Child's Perspective

One of the most important aspects of a child's social map is having a place to call home. In his poem, "The Death of a Hired Hand," Robert Frost wrote of home as the place always there for you, no matter what.[12] H. L. Mencken offered a more formal introduction: "A home is not a mere transient shelter. Its essence lies in its permanence, in its capacity for accretion and solidification, in its quality of representing, in all its details, the personalities of the people who live in it."[13]

The focal point of both Frost's and Mencken's observations is that *home* implies permanence and stability. You have a home when you have a place to go, no matter what. You have a home when you are connected permanently with a place that endures and represents your family. As a young homeless child wrote, "A home is where you can grow flowers if you want."[14]

For young children, the concept of home is closely allied with the concept of family. In fact, for very young children, it is hard to separate the two: "My home is where my family lives." Like turtles, young children carry their homes around with them, as they are carried along by their families. This is important to know. It highlights the importance of social disruption in the lives of parents as a threat to children. Anything that affects the availability of parents and their ability to create and sustain a home for a young child is bad news. Research on children in war zones around the world tells us that young children can cope well with the stress of social upheaval if they retain strong positive attachments to their families, and if parents can continue to project a sense of stability, permanence, and competence to their children.[15] One implication is that when parents of young children have trouble functioning (which may be linked to their sense of being homeless), we can expect negative effects on those children. It is difficult for a family to function well without a home.

Children appreciate being home in new and different ways as they develop. For a child to have a home is for that child to have a family that lives somewhere, that belongs someplace. A family with a home has a place to call its own (putting aside matters like legal ownership, which are virtually meaningless to a child). Such a family may recognize the possibility of moving in the future to another place, but carries with it the expectation that this new place will become a new home.

Why does the young child equate home and family? It follows from the limited ability of young children to engage in abstract thinking. Young children think in concrete terms, and this concrete thinking makes it likely that *home* and *family* will be the same. What about older children? For them, home and family are separable. A friend of our family announced her intention of moving to a new apartment once her daughter graduated from high school and moved on to college. "But I'll never have a home again," her daughter lamented. My own children felt the same way when we moved from one city to another. They had a roof over their heads, yet they felt homeless during the transitional period. I recall with pain suggesting to my twelve-year-old daughter that we "go home" (to the temporary apartment), only to hear her reply, "I have no home."

New home is a shaky concept, a contradiction in terms. This is what my daughter was telling me. For a child to accept a new home is an act of faith. The child is asked to believe that a new place will become a home. Once children leave the period of infancy and early childhood (at approximately age eight), their well-being comes to depend more and more upon social realities beyond the immediate family. Their experiences extend in wider circles beyond the family into the neighborhood and the community. At the same time, home becomes more than family. It includes school, neighborhood, and friends. A new home is thus an expectation of stability, a promise and not a fact. It is a commitment to put down roots, to build relationships, memories, traditions, associations, and images. This is what it means to tell a child that he or she is home in a new house and neighborhood. For a child, home is a crucial feature of the social map, and when it is missing, the child may be set adrift and put in jeopardy.

Child Care

Because children thrive on regularity, change is a challenge to them—particularly if it is rapid and abrupt. Too much change is a threat. A study of child care arrangements conducted in Scandinavia in the 1970s examined the relationship between care arrangements in early childhood and adolescent well-being. The findings were that children did well enough in all kinds of child care patterns, provided there was consistency of care.[16]

Many different configurations of child care can work, so long as they are stable. That's a positive message for families with young children: they don't have to search for the One True Way. Their goal should be to avoid arrangements that are constantly changing, breaking down, or being interrupted. This is one reason why today's families need a supportive community. Many adults are struggling to meet their own individual needs in a community climate that seems to force them to choose between themselves and their children. The result may be child care arrangements that evolve in a haphazard or chaotic way that meets the adults' scheduling needs at the expense of the child's need for stability. As a result, the parents' anger at each other is fueled by day-to-day conflicts, and the resulting negative feelings may spill over to the children.

Of course, some children are more conservative than others, but most children are quite adaptable and resilient if their basic need to feel loved is met. Some children are born into the world with temperaments that increase their risk when exposed to change. One such temperament is best described as *rhythmic*. Babies of rhythmic temperament tick along like clockwork—feeding, sleeping, eliminating, and playing all at regular intervals. Others are more chaotic in their internal regulation. Rhythmic children may be particularly vulnerable to the impact of family instability. When compared with children less dependent on set schedules, rhythmic children involved in parental divorce seem more affected by the change in their family. They are made more uncomfortable by the disruption of routines, of relationships, of everyday life, that comes with the territory of divorce. These children will need extra doses of TLC and structure to help them cope.

Another type of temperament that may affect a child's adjustment to divorce is the *reactive*. Infants of reactive temperament are easily aroused and upset. You walk into their bedrooms and the slightest sound—perhaps the creaking of a floorboard—wakes them up and sets them off. Other babies will sleep right through the intrusion. One of my children was highly reactive; the other was mellow right from the start. Like rhythmic children, those with reactive temperaments will be more vulnerable to the destabilizing experience of divorce.

The Outside Environment

Stability is as much an issue for the environment outside the family as it is for the inner environment of family life. When the social environment around the family becomes unstable, families suffer. We know that this is true when there is massive social breakdown such as occurs in a civil war or economic disaster. For example, during the civil war in the Soviet Union of the 1920s, enormous numbers of children—perhaps eight million—were turned loose by families incapable of caring for them. Similarly, in the Brazil of the 1980s, economic dislocations pushed so many families beyond the brink of breakdown that millions of kids ended up on the street. The United States rarely produces such horrific drama, but it does uproot many children repeatedly and routinely in much more mundane fashion. There are inner-city schools with more than 50 percent turnover each year as families come and go from the neighborhoods the schools serve. Some middle-class suburban areas have similar instability, although it is spread out over several years. Job-related relocations and divorce-related changes in financial status stimulate many of these moves.

What Can We Do?

So what can we do about stability for children? As parents, we can remember its importance in making private decisions about child care. The message is clear. Do all you can to make a good decision *and then stick with it*. One focus of community action ought to be helping parents in this. As a society, we can stabilize child care resources by supporting the professional development of child care providers to reduce turnover. We can set up emergency subsidy funds so that families whose financial situation changes abruptly do not have to change child care arrangements as a consequence.

As citizens, we can support public policies that enhance family stability. Such policies include encouraging businesses to set parental leave policies that allow parents to care for their children without jeopardizing their jobs, and supporting home-health visiting programs that help families get started on the right foot when a new child enters the family. We should also encourage businesses to permit or even reward geographic stability for employees during their childrearing years, particularly during early childhood and adolescence, and to avoid the now-common practice of urging people to transfer from one location to another without regard to their family status. Desirable public policy would make efforts to create a stable housing market, particularly for low-income and lower-middle-class families. It would support social service agencies that respect the child's need for stability, and would plan for permanency in all child welfare decision making, public and private. And it would encourage schools, churches, and private agencies to offer parent education programs to address the need for stability.

Teaching new parents about the attributes of successful families makes a lot of good sense. Premarital counseling is an important place to start teaching these lessons.

Recognizing the importance of stability also means that we recognize the fact that some children have greater vulnerability to instability than others, and that younger children are particularly vulnerable to family disruptions. That implies that we consider the special needs of some children for family stability above all else—including adult needs for change. Early childhood ought to be a period when adults impose a moratorium on change in family arrangements and settle into stable patterns in the child's best interest, postponing relocations, separations, and other upheavals if at all possible until adolescence. Then, as adolescence begins, kids should get to start and finish high school in the same place.

We need laws and policies that require parents (and the courts) to do all they can to avoid unnecessary separation and divorce. When separation and divorce do become inevitable, attention shifts to custody and child support arrangements, and both law and public policy need to make children's sense of security the paramount concern at this point. Some states already require counseling and mediation sessions by law as part of the divorce process. Creating awareness of the intense emotional security needs of children during family crisis is a vital step in our campaign. The preservation of *family* for children, even when marriages end, is crucial. This is not an easy task, of course, but if marital conflict can be separated from the question of joint parental responsibilities, it is doable.

Finding ways to ensure that fathers meet legally mandated child support obligations is another essential piece of this approach. With all the talk these days about *welfare mothers* and *single mothers*, we would do well to remember that the biggest reason why so many mothers are on welfare is the irresponsible behavior of the men who father their children.

Family stability, in the broad sense that I have been discussing it, is the cornerstone of a campaign to combat the problem of social toxicity. Children from stable, successful families face environmental risk from a position of strength. Meeting their needs is made much easier if children operate within stable families. If we start with family stability, the rest of our agenda for dealing with social toxicity comes into focus. If we don't, then children start with one hand tied behind their backs.

Chapter Four

Security

Making Our Kids Safe

A child asks, "Am I safe?" How do we answer?

Security is vitally important for any child's well-being. When children feel safe, they relax. When they relax, they start to explore their environment. You can see this clearly with babies and other very young children. When a parent or other familiar person is around, a child treats the adult as a secure base from which to explore the nearby space. If frightened—perhaps by a loud sound or by the approach of a stranger—the child will quickly retreat to the familiar person.

This pattern is part of normal human development. It is so common that it is used to assess the quality of children's attachment relations. Children who do not use their parents this way—who do not show anxiety when separated and relief when reunited—are thought to have a less-than-adequate attachment relationship (they are called *insecure* or *ambivalent* or *avoidant*). Thus, for very young children, the question of security is relatively simple. As a parent, I remember clearly the physical experience of the clinging, wary child regarding a stranger. And I remember sitting in airports or visiting friends and serving as a secure base for a tiny explorer.

Of course, as children get older, their security needs are transformed. Soon they are getting on school buses and visiting friends' houses by themselves. Eventually they are on the streets at night on their own. But security remains a constant theme for them. Am I safe here? Will I be safe if I go there? Would I be safe then?

Perceiving Danger

Many children do not feel safe. In some cases, their insecurity is grounded in fact: researchers working in inner-city, high-crime neighborhoods report that by age fifteen more than a third of the children have witnessed a homicide.[1] A six-year-old girl once told me that her job was to find her two-year-old sister whenever the shooting started and get her to safety in the bathtub of their apartment. "The bathroom is the safest place," she told me. Being responsible for the safety of another, younger child is a big responsibility for a six-year-old girl. Too big, I think.

For other children, the basis for their sense of insecurity is not life in the urban war zone but just life. A national survey conducted by *Newsweek* and the Children's Defense Fund in 1993 found that only a minority of children nationwide said they felt "very safe" once they walked out the door—most said they only felt "somewhat safe," and about 12 percent said they felt "unsafe."[2] Other surveys report similar results. For example, a Harris poll of sixth to twelfth graders revealed that 35 percent worried they would not live to old age because they would be shot.[3] It is worth giving serious consideration to the question of why even economically secure children in small towns and suburbs feel afraid these days.

More and more children in the United States are experiencing a growing sense of insecurity about the world inside and outside the boundaries of their families. For one thing, they are preoccupied with kidnapping. Teacher after teacher tells me that if he or she asks students what they worry about, kidnapping looms large for most. As noted earlier, one study reported that 43 percent of the elementary school children studied thought it was likely that they would be kidnapped.[4] Having been bombarded with messages of threat via the news and more informal sources (such as worried parents and other well-meaning adults), kids have drawn the logical conclusion: if the adults are so scared, I should be too.

This points to one of the general themes in our understanding of threat of any kind. Children tend to mirror the responses of key adults in their lives. Calm and confident parents and teachers tend to produce confident children who believe the world is manageable. I have seen that in war zones all around the world, and it is clear from clinicians and researchers everywhere. This finding highlights the importance of family and school in creating or undermining a child's sense of security.

Our kids are concerned about family dissolution. To some extent, security equates with stability. Some children ask their parents, "When are you getting divorced?" "When," not "if." They seem to take it for granted that divorce is inevitable, a Sword of Damocles hanging over their heads. The demographics justify their concern. As I mentioned before, Census Bureau data continue to document a divorce rate of about 50 percent. When fears for physical safety are added to family's instability, the net result is a growing sense of insecurity among our children. Recall that one of the important features of a strong family identified in Stennet's research is "ability to deal with crises in a positive manner."[5] And families face many crises today.

It does not take much violence and terror to set a tone of threat. Even in the worst war zones—places like Sarajevo—shooting and killing is intermittent. In the worst high-crime neighborhood, it only takes shots fired a few times a month and homicides a few times a year to create a year-round climate of danger, and to establish insecurity as people's dominant psychological reality. Memory of the emotions of trauma does not decay; it remains fresh. Once you have the feeling of danger, it takes very little new threat to sustain it. For most children in the United States, the world is not as violent as they think it is based upon what they learn to fear. But their fear is real—and to some degree grounded in reality as they see it.

American kids are like little anthropologists. They watch and listen to what goes on around them, and what they are learning from the news, from their favorite television programs, from cartoons, from current events lessons at school, from their parents and aunts and uncles and grandparents is very disturbing. What are they learning about the world? I think that more and more they are learning that the world is a very dangerous place. For some children the level of their fright exceeds the actual dangers they face. For others, the fact of the matter is that they really are surrounded by violence.

The World Is a Dangerous Place

In April 1993, I spent a day in a police car driving around some of the toughest neighborhoods in Philadelphia. The immediate goal of the tactical unit with which I was traveling was to chase down and capture drug dealers and whatever other criminals presented themselves on the streets that day. "We" also staked out a school where a murder suspect was supposed to be coming to pick up his sister—he never showed up. Then we sped around the streets trying to intercept a stolen car that was reportedly heading our way—we never found it.

We staked out a route that the state police thought an armed robbery suspect was taking to an illicit meeting. And we responded to an emergency call on the radio—"officer in trouble, needs backup." The officer in question was alone trying to arrest a couple of kids in a drug bust. When we arrived on the scene the officer was nowhere to be seen, and everyone was afraid he had come to harm—he later turned up a block away, having chased the kids there to make the arrest. At each stop along the way there was an atmosphere of threat, and often outbursts of verbal and physical aggression designed to intimidate and send a message of power to anyone who might challenge the police. And all along the way there were kids watching, taking it all in. Life imitates art. I was living a TV program.

It was unnerving to say the least, this day spent on the front lines of the war against crime. In some ways, it reminded me of the times I have been in a military vehicle in a real war zone. The devastated physical environment certainly did. The bombed-out sections of the poor neighborhoods looked like a war had been fought there. Eventually "we" did catch a drug dealer in the act, and brought him in for processing. While we waited in the detention center as the suspect was booked, my companion asked the police officer if he thought all this arresting did any good. He replied, "No." "What would it take to make a difference?" she asked him. He smiled, formed his right hand into a gun and said, "If I could shoot them as I caught them."

Children of Violence

I thought of this cop and his very understandable frustration a year later, when I met three teenage boys in a prison in North Carolina. I was visiting the prison with an NBC News team—correspondent Stone Phillips, his producer, and the technical crew—to prepare a segment for *Dateline*, a weekly television news magazine. I mainly listened, occasionally offering a line of questioning, as Phillips interviewed the three boys about their lives and the crimes that had put them behind bars.

Ricky was facing a life sentence for killing one of his friends with a stolen pistol while high on drugs. He will probably serve at least twenty years. Larry was facing a twenty-five year term for shooting a police officer while trying to escape arrest for involvement in an armed robbery in which a friend of his stole another kid's jacket. He will probably serve a few years before being released. Charles killed his abusive stepfather and is facing a life sentence. He will probably serve about twenty-five years.

As I sat there listening to the questions and their answers, I was deeply moved and troubled by what I heard and what I saw on the young faces of these boys, all just about my own son's age. Like the policeman who wanted to solve the drug problem by shooting the dealers as he caught them, each of these teenagers in his own way testified to the problem of violence in the lives of American kids—particularly American boys.

One important element in the social toxicity of American culture lies in our acceptance of violence as a technique for punishment, a strategy for dealing with conflict, and a form of entertainment. All this was evident in what the teenagers had to say. Each of them was a living, breathing illustration of the way vulnerable kids succumb to social toxicity. That's what got them to the hard place they occupy today.

Ricky described in detail the physical violence he had experienced and learned at home—a father who assaulted him regularly with his fists, beat him once with a two-by-four, and another time slammed his head against a pool table. I thought of research done by Dorothy Lewis and her colleagues in New York on the role of early neurological damage to kids in the development of chronic aggressiveness. She began by studying kids on death row and found that most of them had experienced serious blows to the head as young children, blows that produced neurological damage that in turn could stimulate rage and reduce the ability to control it.[6]

Here was a kid who had suffered such a biological insult, probably more than once. He came from an extended family with a long tradition of "fighting things out," as he put it. He had bought into the value system that says it is right to punish wrongdoing with violence, as he justified the father who used beatings in place of discipline. At the time of the shooting, he was high on drugs. He shot and killed someone with whom he had fought before, at whose hands he had experienced a prior beating. Ricky is a baby-faced kid who responded to questions with a polite "Yes, sir" or "No, sir," and a wholesome smile. Yet he was extremely vulnerable to the social toxicity of violence.

Larry is a kid from the city, his life almost a caricature of the way the extreme social toxicity of urban life in America can lead to trouble, with the seemingly inexorable pull of guns, televised violence, the drug economy, and the influence of antisocial peers. He seemed singularly unreflective in many ways. When the interviewer asked him if he had any prior experience witnessing or being the victim of violence, he responded, "No, not really." But when asked again in more detail, he acknowledged that he had seen plenty of fights in the neighborhood, and he had seen people cut with knives, and someone once pulled a gun on him and a friend, and he had carried a gun before because "you feel more safe when you have gun with you."

Larry reminded me of a man I met in Northern Ireland once who was taking great pains to describe the positive character of his society to offset the bad publicity of sectarian bombings and shootings that are commonly referred to as The Troubles. He told me he was a good example because, "The Troubles haven't touched me." And then he proceeded to tell me that he had been on the scene of three bombings, had his truck hijacked three times by armed gunmen, and once had been pulled from the cab of his truck, knocked unconscious, and held at gunpoint for failing to give the proper respect at an IRA roadblock.

Larry reported that, yes, he watched a lot of movies with violence and that his favorite TV program was *Cops*, but insisted that "it never done nothing to me." And here he sat imprisoned for shooting a cop. He had lived out a common movie fantasy of escaping in a hail of bullets but he insisted that his crime was "the first time shooting somebody."

Larry saw his imprisonment as a bit of bad luck, and he seemed genuinely puzzled by his behavior. When asked about his twin brother and his friends, he said he expected they would end up in trouble and find their way to prison. When he is released in the next couple of years, he will be surprised to find himself shooting someone again. I won't. Larry has internalized the social toxicity of violence without reflection, as if it went right to his behavior without being processed by his mind.

Charles presented a story as sad as any. The stepfather he killed sounds like what my Italian father used to call a "low life." Charles' stepfather was a physically big man—6'5"—with a bully's small meanness. I listened as Charles laid out the excruciating details of unremitting and unrelenting verbal and physical abuse. He chronicled the futile efforts of probation officers to intervene, of his own efforts to live with his grandparents, and the mounting sense of inevitability of "doing what I had to do." One night, Charles came home to his drunken stepfather, loaded a rifle, and shot him in the head at point-blank range.

Two days earlier, he said, he reached the "last straw" when he witnessed his stepfather casually smack Charles' two-year-old nephew across the face, bloodying the child's mouth. "I couldn't take it anymore," Charles said. "I did what I had to do." Were there any alternatives for Charles? Not as far as he could see. "What was I supposed to do?" he asked. "I put up with it for two years!" And now he sits in prison, twice a victim: of the family abuse that produced so much pain and rage, and of the social toxicity of the culture that told him clearly that when you are faced with such a problem you're on your own. It told him almost in so many words, "We have no alternatives for you but violence." This makes Charles' act a form of self-defense. Boys seem particularly prone to learn this lesson. But increasingly, we see evidence that girls are falling prey as well.

A few years ago, I was approached by a lawyer in Milwaukee to serve as an expert witness in the case of a teenage girl accused of murdering another girl. Mary (not her real name) had apparently shot and killed the girl on the street as part of an attempt to steal her jacket. This shooting came as the culmination of a string of incidents characterized by escalating violence. To prepare myself for the case, I read the lengthy transcripts of interviews conducted with Mary as well as summaries of reports compiled by human service agencies and schools as background for the judge.

Mary's life was an appalling amalgam of what it means to grow up in a violent society. She had been raped, she had been beaten up on the street several times, her mother abused her physically, and five members of her extended family were killed in the years preceding her own foray into homicide. Mary suffered from all the psychological and moral consequences of trauma and these forces conspired together to place her on trial for first-degree murder.

Her case attracted a modicum of attention in the mass media because it involved two girls, because the precipitating incident (the jacket) was so trivial in the great scheme of things, and because the case epitomized the growing problem of teen street violence. Beyond these concerns, of course, it represented for me the problem of social toxicity in its most virulent form: a vulnerable child growing up in a weak, violent, and destabilized family embedded in a dangerous community incapable of providing basic emotional and physical security. In this, she is not alone.

A few days after I met the boys in North Carolina, I visited a therapeutic day school for emotionally disturbed children and adolescents in Chicago. The director had asked me to pay them a visit to look things over and then sit down with the staff to discuss my observations. Why? Because he and the rest of the staff had noticed an increasing level of aggressive disturbance in the kids attending the school. The director founded the school in 1970, and has plenty of experience with troubled kids. But the current crop, he said, was "something else." They seemed more aggressive than previous classes, and the staff was worried, both for them and about them.

I visited three classrooms that day. The first was for kids between eight and twelve. The second contained kids between eleven and fourteen. The third had kids up to fifteen. What was striking about these children was the nastiness of the boys, the aggressiveness of their language, their posture, and their imagery. Verbal insults to me, to the staff, and to each other were almost nonstop. Among one of the groups, the half-hour visit ended with two of the boys being removed from the classroom because of escalating aggressive words, gestures, and posturing, culminating in kicking books and furniture, and threatening to punch a teacher. It was exhausting, and very disturbing.

For the brief time I was able to talk with the kids, I asked them about television and video games and other features of modern cultural life in our society. Even the youngest group—so many of whom still had the appearance of children—were absorbed with the imagery of violence from movies and television and video games. It was unrelenting. The most virulently violent images fascinated and aroused them. I had seen it before—too often before. It is one of the truisms among those who work with troubled kids in America that they are hooked on the violent culture, so these kids were nothing out of the ordinary in that regard.

When they talked about real life, it was hardly better. Child after child spoke about witnessing violent incidents—a brother shot, a cousin committing suicide, an attempted rape, a dog tortured to death, a parent killed. Their emotional disturbance screened much of what might be on their minds. I had to find out something of their stories from the teachers and other staff members later. But that was not the point as I see it here and now.

What These Children Can Tell Us

Before coal mining became high tech, it was standard practice for miners to bring caged canaries into the mines with them and hang the cages from the roof beams of the tunnels. Why? The canaries were an advance warning system for the buildup of toxic gasses in the mine. When a bird stopped singing and died, the miners knew there was danger. Similarly, the most vulnerable kids in our society serve as weather vanes and social indicators of what is going on. They are our canaries. And they are dying.

In 1951, the United States was in the midst of the polio epidemic. Parents worried particularly at the onset of summer when the risk was greatest. I remember that. There was a national mobilization to respond, and the Salk vaccine was a consequence that eventually eliminated polio as a threat. But note this. In 1993, more children were killed in acts of violence in the United States than ever died from polio in any year of the epidemic.

Violence is the new epidemic, and the emotionally disturbed kids I spent the day with in Chicago were another manifestation of what I had seen a couple of days earlier at the prison in North Carolina. These kids were more of the vulnerable ones, the high-risk kids who were displaying something fundamental about the culture in which all of us live. They were showing what they have learned from their personal experiences with violence in their families and in their neighborhoods, and in their culture, our culture: the hard-edged language, the wallowing in the often grotesque imagery of violence that was dished up to them daily on the screens of their television sets. And I could see the viciousness of the cycle in which they were caught.

I could imagine being in their parents' shoes, tempted to bail out from a child such as this, to capitulate to television watching—anything to avoid having to deal with the stress the children radiated. But the cost is limitless—to the child, to the family, to the society—when parents allow themselves to retreat from active efforts to socialize these children.

These kids are ready to be armed, and our society is prepared to offer them guns. Maybe not today, but soon. And then, God help us. When asked why he carried a gun, one of the boys in the North Carolina prison said he was scared and carrying a gun made him feel safer. When I asked a nine-year-old boy in a California housing project what it would take to make him feel safer there, his only response was, "If I had a gun of my own." The week I sat down to work on this chapter an eleven-year-old boy in Chicago shot and killed a fourteen-year-old girl, then a few days later was himself killed by fellow gang members who feared he would reveal their secrets if he was apprehended.

The problem of violence in our society is truly pervasive in its scope and cancerous in its nature. It infects our institutional life and our community life, and it drives the dark side of our culture. And more and more, it is an inescapable and highly influential fact of life in understanding childhood in America. We get used to it. We adjust. We lower our expectations.

Like fish asked to describe water, we have difficulty describing what is around us—and often within us—because we have nothing with which to compare it. Unless we can travel to other places where violence is not the endemic cultural medium it is for us, we may never notice. Indeed. During the staff meeting at the school for emotionally disturbed kids, I asked one of the teachers how she felt when one of the boys raised his fist to her. At first she looked puzzled, as if she didn't remember the incident. Then the light of recognition dawned. "I guess I didn't notice it," she said. "You get used to it when it happens all the time."

But these vulnerable kids show us clearly what is out there— and in here. Every message they live out in their crimes and in their aggressiveness is a message we all receive; we breathe it in every day. We live in a violent society. It is tempting to think that the violence in our society only affects the most vulnerable among us: Ricky, Larry, Charles, Mary, and other boys and girls like them. But that comforting belief would be a mistake. These kids may act out violently, but they are not alone. Gangs are cropping up in the suburbs. There are documented reports of middle-class teenagers carrying weapons to school. I spoke with a third-grade class in a middle-class suburb in which a third of the children told me they knew where to get a gun "if they needed one."

All this came to mind one night as I sat watching *Masterpiece Theater* on public television with my then eleven-year-old daughter. It was the concluding episode of a British series about a nun who had left the convent to run her family's business. A recently fired ex-employee showed up at the factory, drunk and full of vindictive rage. As he approached the building in front of which stood the nun and several co-workers, my daughter turned to me and said, "He's going to blow them away!" This peaceful child anthropologist was offering up her conclusions about conflict resolution American style. I doubt she will ever act out the violence she understands is a working principle of American life because she and her life have been spared the risk factors of Larry, Ricky, Charles, and Mary. But the social toxicity has crept into her consciousness nonetheless. In her own way, she is a product of life in a violent society.

The Violent Society

Homicide data paint a stark picture: the United States is a world leader. The only countries that rival us are profoundly distressed societies like Colombia, where murder is linked to the enormity of the illicit drug industry (as it is here too). What you might call the demography of violence tells an increasingly sad tale for children and growing up in the 1990s.

Millions of American children not only watch violence on television, but face the challenge of having to live with chronic community violence. Since 1974, the rate of serious assault (potentially lethal assaults with knives and guns) has increased 400 percent in Chicago, and other metropolitan areas reveal similar patterns. In interviews with families living in public housing projects in Chicago, we learned that virtually all the children have firsthand experience with shooting by the time they are five years old, and that mothers spontaneously identify shooting as their biggest fear for children.[7]

Other surveys have revealed that more than a third of the kids living in high-crime neighborhoods have witnessed a homicide by the time they are fifteen years old, and more than 70 percent have witnessed a serious assault. You can visit a junior high school and ask, "How many of you have been to at least one funeral for a kid who was killed?" and virtually all the kids will raise their hands.

These figures are much more like the experience of kids in the war zones I have visited in other countries than they are of what we should expect for children like ours, who are living in peace. Indeed, when I traveled to Northern Ireland a few years ago, I appreciated that I was entering a war zone, and verified that shortly after leaving the airport. On the road to Belfast, I came upon the site of a shooting that had occurred not more than fifteen minutes earlier. A Protestant had killed a Catholic, or vice versa. During my stay, there were bombings and further shootings.

But when I returned to Chicago and computed the relative risk to children here versus in Northern Ireland, I realized something dreadful: the odds of a child being killed here are fifteen times what they are over there, and that was before the IRA cease-fire announced in September 1994. If an inner-city parent were to come to me and say, "Can you tell me something concrete and specific I could do to make my child safer?" I could reply with confidence, "Move to Northern Ireland."

The litany of statistics continues to mount. In 1982, in Chicago, 32 percent of homicides were committed in public—thus becoming part of the community experience, an experience that many children see and hear firsthand. In 1993, 67 percent of the homicides (and there were significantly more of them) were committed in public.[8] And these extreme data for big cities are more and more being matched by an upsurge of street violence in smaller cities and towns. I recently learned of drive-by shootings taking place in Battle Creek, Michigan, home of Kellogg's Cornflakes.

Because of improved medical trauma technology, many of the young victims of shootings and stabbings stay out of the homicide statistics. But many of them end up with permanent disabilities, and the physical rehabilitation centers are filling up with young wounded men just as they did in the 1970s, when an earlier generation was being shipped home from Southeast Asia as casualties of a different war. And the statistics on community violence do not give the entire story. There is also a story to be told about the interior experience of violence and trauma for America's children, a story that revolves around three dark secrets.

Snowden's Secret

The first of these three secrets I call Snowden's Secret, referring to Joseph Heller's book, *Catch-22*.[9] *Catch-22* tells the story of American bomber crews during World War II. The central character, Yossarian, has undergone a traumatic experience, learning what he calls Snowden's Secret. During one of their missions, Yossarian receives a message over the intercom that another member of the crew—Snowden—has been hit by antiaircraft fire. When he goes to help Snowden and opens his flak jacket, Snowden's insides fall out on the floor.

This is Snowden's secret, that the human body, which appears so firm and durable, is really only a fragile bag filled with gooey stuff and lumps, suspended precariously on a very fragile skeleton. Violence reveals this secret, and it is traumatic in the sense of being an experience that changes you forever. You never fully recover from it. It requires all of your emotional, spiritual, and philosophical resources to cope with Snowden's Secret, as people who work in emergency rooms or who investigate automobile crashes or who travel to war zones will attest. I certainly will.

Children learn Snowden's Secret from experiencing—or witnessing—violence, when the human body meets bullets and knives. And I believe this process of witnessing need not be firsthand. When I traveled to Kuwait at the end of the Gulf War on behalf of UNICEF, I interviewed kids who had learned Snowden's Secret. They had seen atrocities—shootings, hangings, beatings. Some of them had unwittingly brought down violent trauma upon themselves, like the boys I met who had played with a hand grenade until it exploded and tore open the chest of a cousin. Many of these children were experiencing post-traumatic stress disorder (PTSD), the package of symptoms that arises from encountering trauma and being changed by the experience.

PTSD symptoms in children include sleep disturbances, daydreaming, recreating trauma in play, extreme startle responses, and diminished expectations for the future. And there is growing evidence that PTSD may disrupt the chemical balance in the child's brain—the child's neurochemistry. Put simply, this evidence suggests that trauma due to loss and violence can alter the balance between the neurochemicals that help people regulate their behavior and maintain a positive orientation to life (most notably serotonin) and the neurochemicals that are associated with arousal of feelings including aggression (norepinephrine).[10] Thus, trauma can produce significant psychological problems that interfere with learning and appropriate social behavior in school and that also interfere with normal parent-child relationships.

That these Kuwaiti children were experiencing PTSD was no surprise. What was a bit surprising, however, was that a year later, when more systematic follow-up research was conducted, another group of Kuwaiti children was identified as demonstrating PTSD symptoms. These children had not witnessed any atrocities firsthand. What had happened to them was that they had been shown videotapes of Iraqi atrocities in an effort to teach them, to indoctrinate them politically about the origins and meaning of the Iraqi invasion. And seeing the atrocities on TV had an unfortunate side effect—they had learned Snowden's Secret by remote control instead of firsthand.

I thought of these children one day when I was visiting a first-grade classroom in Chicago. A little girl named Gloria brought up her "Birthday Book" to show me. The book began nicely enough—"Happy Birthday," read the first page. But then began a visual litany of all the reasons why children didn't have birthdays, because they were shot, because they were stabbed, because they were beheaded, because they were disemboweled, because they were kidnapped. I wondered with worry about the source of this flood of traumatic imagery. What had happened to this little girl that she should tell this story?

After some investigation, it became clear what had happened. When her mother went out, she left Gloria in the care of her teenage cousins, who sat her down in front of their favorite movies—*Nightmare on Elm Street, Halloween,* and the other slasher films that are so popular with American adolescents. But for Gloria these films—and the image of Freddy Krueger in particular—

were traumatic. She was learning Snowden's Secret from an expert. If one were trying to design a character specifically for the purpose of traumatizing young children, Freddy Krueger would be nearly ideal. He can't be killed, so he always comes back. He enters into the dreams of his victims, so you can't protect yourself by asserting the distinction between fantasy and reality. And he kills in a particularly vivid manner, with the finger knives that adorn his hands.

Informal surveys indicate a substantial proportion of young children know him. Several years ago, one count reported that 15 percent of the first graders reported having seen at least one of his movies. Whenever I go into elementary school classrooms, I find he is well known. A policeman in Chicago once reported that he had done a survey of eighth graders and found that 85 percent said they had recently been to see an R-rated violent movie, and further that 55 percent of the time they were accompanied by a younger child. From my perspective, teaching kids about Snowden's Secret through movie characters like Freddy Krueger is like teaching sex education by showing kids hard-core pornography. Learning Snowden's Secret is a threat to children, one that this mode of instruction compounds. But Snowden's is only one of the secrets children learn from witnessing violence. There is another secret, perhaps even more disturbing.

Dantrell's Secret

Dantrell Davis was a little boy who lived in Chicago until the fall of 1992. One morning his mother walked him to school. His teachers were waiting on the steps of the school, and there were cops on the corner. And yet, as he walked the seventy-five feet between his mother and the school he was shot in the back of the head and killed. His death sends an important message to other children: adults can't protect you; you are on your own.

If Snowden's Secret teaches children something disturbing about the human body, Dantrell's Secret teaches them something at least equally disturbing about the social fabric, and about adult authority in particular. It teaches children that you may be left alone in the face of threat. Alone.

One of the truisms of research on children growing up in war zones around the world is that the first line of defense against fear and trauma is parental protection. As one observer put it after examining children in England during World War II, "children measure the danger that threatens them chiefly by the reactions of those around them, especially by their trusted parents and teachers."[11] This has certainly been my experience traveling to a dozen war zones around the world in the last decade.

Children enter into a social contract with adults. The terms of this contract are roughly these: I will obey and trust you, and in return you will protect and care for me. Dantrell's Secret voids this contract. Once I visited a little boy who lived in a refugee camp. Months earlier he had learned Dantrell's Secret. Soldiers had come into the camp looking for someone. With the boy's mother standing next to him a soldier grabbed the boy and put a knife to his throat. "Tell me where Omar is," he said to the mother, "or I'll cut your boy's throat." That this could happen to him while his mother stood powerless was the most traumatic element of the experience.

It doesn't always take such dramatic incidents to teach Dantrell's Secret. I visited a Cambodian displaced persons camp in Thailand a few years ago. What struck me was how hideous it was for mothers. Men played a marginal role—often disappearing for long periods back into Cambodia to fight in the civil war. The future was uncertain—no one knew when, if ever, families would return to their homeland. There was a high level of domestic violence in the camp, and weapons abounded. Finally, the moderating influence of the outside world departed at 5 P.M. every day, when the international workers left and the camps were under the control of gangs.

Not surprisingly, this environment produced high levels of maternal depression. A recent survey had reported that 50 percent of the mothers were seriously depressed. Perhaps the only question was why it wasn't 100 percent! But depressed mothers have some predictable consequences for children. Children of depressed mothers tend to receive inadequate adult supervision—and thus are more likely to be injured in accidents. And so it was, according to a pediatrician who worked in the camp, that the children were always getting run over, drowning in the irrigation ditches, burning themselves up, or getting hurt playing with weapons they found. And these same depressed mothers were psychologically unavailable to help children deal with the stresses and potentially traumatic events they encountered.

I thought of these Cambodian mothers again when a week later I had occasion to visit a public housing project in Chicago. The parallels were striking. Here too men were in marginal roles, always disappearing to escape the police, the welfare authorities, or some conflict with a rival group or individual in the neighborhood. The future was uncertain, and there was a high level of domestic violence. Weapons were abundant—and used. And here too gangs were in control after 5 P.M. when the social workers and teachers representing the outside world went home.

So it came as no surprise that when a research group in New Orleans conducted a mental health survey in a similar public housing project they discovered that 50 percent of the mothers were seriously depressed.[12] They also found that 40 percent of the mother-child attachment relationships in the first year of life were disrupted (or *disorganized*, to use the investigators' term).

Such an environment is precisely suited to increase the traumatic nature of violent experiences. Without parents actively in charge, children learn Dantrell's Secret and have it reinforced daily. And what do these children do to cope with the knowledge that they have to fend for themselves, because they are on their own in a dangerous environment? I think they cope as best they can, and this includes banding together in gangs for protection. As a boy in Michigan once told me, "If I join a gang, I'm 50 percent safe. If I don't join a gang, I'm 0 percent safe." Adults just don't figure into the equation.

Milgrim's Secret

The third secret learned by children exposed to traumatic violence is what I call "Milgrim's Secret." The reference here is to psychologist Stanley Milgrim's research on the willingness of normal adults to inflict torture on others if they are ordered to do so or believe there is some other justification.[13]

Milgrim's Secret is that when it comes to violence, "anything is possible." An adult survivor of child abuse reported the following incident. The police were called once when she was a child to investigate reports that her mother was beating her. When the police interviewed the child she denied that her mother beat her. Later, her mother asked her why she didn't tell the police about the beating. She looked at her mother and said, "Because you could kill me." Milgrim's Secret: *anything* is possible. Children learn it, and they and the larger community are jeopardized by that learning. Alongside threats of death are the more common phenomena of a childhood lived in the shadow of domestic violence—the "respected civic leader" who beats his wife, the charming mother who humiliates her child, the admired high school athlete who beats up his younger siblings. Anything is possible.

The Costs of Adjusting to Violent Trauma

Living with violent trauma is costly for a child. PTSD makes the child struggle to get through the day—and the night as well, since repetitive dreams are a common symptom. The result is a child who is increasingly prone to disruption by further loss and trauma and who may become more negative in outlook and behavior.

Early exposure to violent trauma can also make kids prime candidates for involvement in gangs, where the violent economy of the illicit drug trade offers a sense of belonging and solidarity—and also a cash income—for kids who have few pro-social alternatives for either. Another result is that children and youth have diminished prospects for the future. Violent trauma reduces a child's confidence in life, his or her belief that life will be long. Among a group of children kidnapped and buried underground in their school bus, a year later there was a significant decrease—six years—in the children's reporting of how long they expected to live.[14]

In the intense form it takes among kids exposed to chronic violent trauma, this tendency may lead to terminal thinking, evident when you ask a fifteen-year-old what he expects to be when he is thirty and he answers, "Dead." This lack of a positive future orientation produces depression, rage, and disregard for human life— their own and others. It also undermines motivation to participate in the investment activities of adolescence, such as staying in school or doing homework, or to avoid high-risk behaviors such as unprotected sex, carrying weapons, and joining the drug trade. When learned together, Snowden's, Dantrell's, and Milgrim's Secrets offer a potent recipe for personal and social destruction, and one that speaks loudly about the children's interior experience of violence and trauma.

Information collated by the National Research Council in 1992 indicates that patterns of aggression are so well established by age eight that without intervention they then become predictive of patterns of aggression at age thirty-eight.[15] The kids whom peers at age eight name as the ones who hit and push and bully and shove and kick and bite and fight, are the adults who hit family members, get into fights in the community, and drive their cars aggressively.

I view the violent upheaval in Los Angeles and other cities as a devastating reminder of the fragility of community life—as a social heart attack. Much as a physical heart attack serves as a warning that something is wrong in the body, a social heart attack tells us something is wrong in the community. We ignore these warnings at our peril. There are self-serving, antisocial individuals and groups in our society prepared to mobilize and exploit the anger, alienation, and hostility that many kids feel.

Recall that Machiavelli wrote his cynical political tract *The*

Prince soon after being imprisoned and abused by the government of his city.[16] Traumatic experiences create a fertile field for nasty political and religious beliefs and organizations. The personal history of terrorists, religious fanatics, gangsters, killers, and authoritarian bigots often reveals a similar pattern that combines traumatic experiences of violence coupled with social exploitation and oppression. These individuals are the canaries who tell us how bad the social toxins are in the environment. Others show milder variants that because of fortunate family experiences or special individual resilience or effective professional intervention do not deteriorate into full-blown criminal violence in the home, on the streets, or in the workplace.

The links are forged early. If we don't disengage them early, we are likely to witness adolescent aggression that becomes the stuff of which serious criminal violence is made. And if things get that far it may take years, even decades, in a closely controlled environment to accomplish the two-fold task of protection and rehabilitation.

Transformational Grace

A day after I rode with the police in Philadelphia, I spent some time in a state penitentiary visiting with a group of men serving life sentences for murder—in some cases more than one murder. Among these ten men, virtually all had spent more than half their lives behind bars. Many had been sentenced to life imprisonment as teenagers and now fifteen or twenty years later they were full-grown men, my age peers, only I was visiting and they were not going anywhere. A day before I had been riding with the police who were looking for the nephews, children, younger brothers, and cousins of these lifers. But today I sat with them, and I began to see a whole new realm of human potential.

As we talked, a picture emerged of transformation—spiritual, educational, philosophical, and psychological. The passage of time had brought a less explosive neurochemistry and perhaps even a measure of wisdom. These men had spent their time usefully. As an experiment in human development, it seemed to have succeeded. The irony, of course, was that Pennsylvania law did not permit parole of life sentences. Unless there was some drastic gubernatorial intervention in the form of a commutation of sentence, these men were likely to spend the rest of their days where they were. And yet they had changed.

It was hopeful, this idea that violent kids like the ones I met in North Carolina could become men like these. I'm sure that meeting any one of these people on the street in their youth would have made for a very frightening experience. And yet here and now the feeling was one of assurance, even inspiration. They had read books and attended classes and counseling. They had reached for some spiritual meaning beyond the rotten contours of their preprison lives. And they had changed. The change was real, not put on for the interview; the warden of the prison assured me of that.

I thought of what psychoanalyst Alice Miller calls *transformational grace*.[17] Some of these men had it, this transformational grace that allows a person to become more and better than a victim or a perpetrator. I was uplifted by their development, no matter how discouraging it was to know that it might never get them released. The warden spoke of his reliance on these men to help make the prison run smoothly and as humanely as possible.

The men represented something important in our efforts to understand violence and trauma in human development and in American life. With newfound voices, these men were telling me about where violence came into their lives, how they had swallowed it whole, and how it had devoured them.

As I sat with these men in the prison, I thought of a visit to my office earlier that month from two young men who were participants in the international group "Children of War." One was a Cambodian—Arn Chorn—who had survived the genocidal regime of Pol Pot's Khmer Rouge. But he had survived at great psychic and moral cost. Symptoms of PTSD were with him still (as they are for many Cambodian survivors) and he suffered pangs of guilt for the nasty things he had done to survive in a situation in which scruples could prove fatal.

Sitting with Arn Chorn in my office was Jacob—a young African-American man from New York who had heard the Cambodian speak about what it was like to grow up in Cambodia under the Khmer Rouge, and drew the parallels to his own experiences growing up in the war zone of the inner city. Jacob too suffered from PTSD. And he too had done despicable things to survive.

But like Arn, Jacob had triumphed through a process of psychological and moral transformation. These two young men were different people now that they had crossed over a great human divide. They had come back from the killing fields and were committed to telling their story, telling of what they had seen and done and heard and learned from the experience. Both were wounded, as are most victims of post-traumatic stress disorder. But both testified to the potential for human regeneration that is our great hope.

I think often of Arn and Jacob, and the three teenagers in the North Carolina prison, and the ten men in the Pennsylvania prison, and the college student I know who crossed over into the world of violence but found his way back, and the many other traumatized kids I've met. I think of them as I see and hear more about the growing social toxicity of violence in American life, in the experience of American children.

I have spoken with the most vulnerable and seen how poisoned they have become. I have listened to some who have recovered. They can teach us important lessons about violence and trauma. They show us that committing acts of violence is traumatic. They show us that witnessing acts of violence is traumatic. And they show us that inside most of the adolescent and adult perpetrators of violence are traumatized children, untreated children, frightened children.

Right now it is only the most vulnerable among our children who display fully the bitter fruits of living in a violent society. But each year the number of vulnerable children, youth, families, and communities grows. Each year the level of social toxicity associated with violence and trauma increases. While we still have a society to work with, I think we must mount a sustained national campaign to reduce childhood experience of the legitimacy of aggression, to heal the trauma of kids already victimized, to control and transform young perpetrators, and to detoxify the social environment for all of us.

Given the level of violence brought into our homes by the mass media and the level of violence in our society, it is no wonder that our children do not feel safe and that we worry about keeping them safe. Worst of all, the need for security—theirs and ours—can lead us to strategies that actually legitimize and increase aggression and violence in our families and our communities as we mistakenly fight fire with fire. But that's a self-defeating path. Recall Buddha's words: "You will not be punished for your anger, you will be punished by your anger." Or, as Wayne Dyer puts it in his book *Real Magic*, "All that you fight weakens you, all that you support empowers you."[18]

What Can We Do?

Here are some strategies that can get us started toward decreasing aggression and violence: you can regulate television and movie watching. Monitor what children do watch and how they reflect what they watch in their clothing, their language, and the way they treat each other. Encourage positive media experiences, positive language, and positive peer relations.

Use positive discipline, discipline that teaches love and self-control. Avoid using violence to discipline children. As Murray Straus points out in his book *Beating the Devil Out of Them*, all physical punishment causes problems later on in life.[19] It's often hard to see the connection at the lower end of the spectrum—so-called normal spanking—but there is a connection. Instead, recognize that alternatives to hitting do exist, and that they work without the nasty side effects. Start early with using words to set limits, impose real understandable consequences, and apply them consistently. But always remember that verbal abuse is at least as destructive as physical abuse and often is even worse in its consequences. The key is unconditional love, acceptance, and kindness. That's the best way to establish a climate in which effective (but nonviolent) discipline can flourish.

You can join together with other parents so that you all enforce the same expectations for behavior and TV watching. The more there is a consensus among parents in a school, a child care center, or a neighborhood, the easier it is to get compliance from kids. Here's a place where individualism makes things more difficult. Look to the PTA, the churches, and other groups for leadership and support.

You can work to make schools safety zones for children. Work with educators to make schools smaller so they can exert more personalized and thus effective discipline and avoid guns and gangs. Parent volunteers in the hallways can help create a positive social climate in the school. Support violence prevention and conflict resolution programs at all levels—from the preschool to the high school—to remake the culture of childhood and adolescence.

In addition, you can involve children and youth in lobbying efforts to promote gun control and disarmament. These efforts help persuade kids that adults are strong and are strongly committed to safety and security. All these efforts can help transform the culture of childhood and ultimately detoxify the social environment.

Chapter Five

Affirmation and Acceptance

Creating Identity for Children

A child's sense of identity arises out of messages about self received from all quarters—parents, teachers, and culture, as well as from personal introspection. It has an individual and a collective dimension. Thus, each child (as well as each adult) has an identity as a separate person and as a member of various groups. I am American, male, psychologist, father, lover, son, brother, friend, and earthling, depending upon the point of reference. Knowing who you are is important. And affirmation of that knowledge is of greatest importance.

Identity is an important resource, a source of strength, a basis for resilience in coping with the world. It is an important element in the "social map" described in Chapter Two. And a child's social map is both a product and a cause of behavior and development. The map reflects the child's experience and competence, and motivates and guides the child in ways that influence the course of development.

One way the map does this is by leading the child to further experiences. These experiences, in turn, reinforce or redirect the child's social map. That's why positive identity is central to resilience and negative identity compounds risks posed by the social environment. A student of mine described to me how pride in his heritage gave him the strength he needed to overcome the adversity he faced as a child living in a poor, dangerous neighborhood. As an illiterate and fatherless 13-year-old drug dealer, he had cut down another kid with a shotgun in a war over turf. Yet within a few years, he had been able to transform his consciousness and find the resources to rebuild his life. In my classroom at Cornell University, moving and penetrating analytic essays poured from his pen.

On the other hand, a colleague working in a prison described how a convicted murderer once told her, "I'd rather be wanted for murder than not be wanted at all." Everyone searches for meaning.

Acceptance, Affirmation, and Accountability

Children thrive on acceptance and wither when they are rejected, because acceptance and rejection affect identity, the very definition of who they are. Appreciation feeds the development of a strong, positive self-concept; it is a characteristic of strong families and successful children. Rejection, on the other hand, is what anthropologist Roland Rohner calls a "psychological malignancy;" it eats away at self-worth.[1] Rejected children and youth are in jeopardy. They are prone to antisocial and self-destructive behavior as well as to the formation of negative self-concepts. Rejected children draw social maps in which they are insignificant specks or are surrounded by enemies, and these maps justify and encourage preemptive hostility.

In facing a toxic social environment, a strong, positive identity is crucial. At stake is pride in who you are as an individual and as part of a group. But where does such an identity come from? How does a child learn that he or she is valued? Family provides the single most important training ground, creating situations in which children can conclude that they are valuable. This process requires more than telling children, "You are wonderful." It requires *showing* children that they are wonderful.

Children need to find evidence of their worth in both word and deed. In *Maggie's American Dream*, African-American child psychiatrist James Comer offers a biography of his mother and his family as an example of child development under conditions of great social risk.[2] He asks why he and his siblings all succeeded in life though they were black and poor and faced a racist society. His answer has multiple elements, but one strong theme is the role of affirmation and identity.

James Comer and his siblings were taught they were people of worth, people who could be and should be held accountable for their behavior. This linking of affirmation with accountability is crucial. In a sense, acceptance lies in being taken seriously and treated as a competent person. Most of us come to learn that being taken seriously means being given a chance to succeed, not being handed success on a silver platter.

In a moving passage, Comer asks his mother to speak of his father. "They don't make men like that any more," she says, "except, of course, for his sons."[3] The message of affirmation and identity is clear, and it clearly comes with expectations for behavior: "Because you are valuable, I expect you to live up to the high standards set by your father." And James Comer's mother backed up her words by investing her time and energy in making sure her children attended school, did their homework, met their commitments, and generally kept up their end of the social contract.

We hear the term *self-esteem* in parenting and educational circles a great deal. But self-esteem is a conclusion children draw upon themselves. The evidence for this conclusion must be found in relationships, achievement, spiritual development, and competence, as well as in smiles, hugs, and kind words. Many children suffer from a lack of affirmation in this positive sense of themselves drawn from encounters with challenge and accountability. Mere assertions of worth can seem hollow to a child unless backed up with action.

How can we help families meet the challenge of affirmation and identity? As parents, we can appreciate the lessons that James Comer learned from his mother. We can strive to communicate that we value our children and therefore expect great things of them. The precise nature of those things depends on their individual talents and interests, of course, as well as on what their immediate environment offers in the way of opportunities.

This attention to the child's interests is what differentiates genuine affirmation from artificial pressure. Children who are following their own talents and interests do not need pushing. They only need facilitating assistance from parents who recognize accomplishment and provide access to resources. My son is a jazz saxophonist. My daughter is a horsewoman. These identities arose from following the paths their talents opened up for them. What they needed from me and from their mother was a saxophone and a horse, clear messages that what they were pursuing was valuable, and a family climate in which they were told and shown that they were loved and valued. Opportunity and affirmation lead to positive identity.

And what if you can't afford a saxophone or riding lessons? The key is to do the best with what you have. When I was a child, money was in short supply, but I had a dream of becoming a ball player, and my dad took the time to help me learn the game by hitting fly balls for me. My mother put in hours helping me do my homework so I could become a good student. Every child wants to be something. The most important parental investments are time, energy, and acceptance.

The Effects of Television

TV immerses children in a collective culture of commercial, athletic, political, and entertainment images. Too much of this, and children start to base their identities on what they see on the tube, rather than on what they do for themselves and derive from their relationships with the people around them. There is a phoniness to these feeble identities when contrasted with the kind of self that arises from genuine face-to-face interaction.

What is more, early research on the introduction of television into families revealed evidence of suppressed family interaction, which is tantamount to suppressing support and character development. A 1951 study found that 78 percent of the respondents

indicated no conversation occurring during viewing except at specific times such as commercials. The researcher saw it this way:
"The nature of the family social life during a program could be
described as 'parallel' rather than interactive, and the set does seem
quite clearly to dominate family life when it is on."[4] Now, with most
households having at least two televisions, this effect may well be
even more pronounced, and Marie Winn was correct when she
referred to television as "the plug-in drug."[5]

Another study done in the mid 1950s revealed that even then
36 percent of the respondents said that television viewing was the
only family activity they participated in during the week.[6] By now
that figure appears to be much higher. Maccoby's study of parents
before and after the addition of television to the household also
reported that in response to the question "Has TV made it easier or
harder to take care of the child at home?", 54 percent said "easier,"
33 percent said "no difference," and only 3 percent said "harder."
But "easier" clearly meant a decrease in interaction: 62 percent of
the mothers said "TV keeps the children quiet." As one mother put
it, "It's much easier—it's like putting him to sleep."[7] But it's disturbing to think about just what that child might have been dream-
ing while "asleep" in front of the television. . . .

Television viewing now shapes and changes the social environment of children from the word go. The change is in the direction of less interaction, and interaction is the stuff of which human
character and relationships are made. A decade after television was
introduced, Urie Bronfenbrenner began to detect declining interaction between children and parents.[8] As time doing things with
adults declines, the impact of what children see and hear from television increases. This is a particularly vicious cycle.

Big Schools and the Problem of Being Marginal

After what happens in their homes, the biggest influence on children's identities is the school they attend. And it is here that we

have a genuine opportunity to improve life for our teenagers. In my observation, big high schools are the greatest single threat the adolescent community faces. Big schools encourage spectatorship, and exclude all but a tiny proportion of their students from leadership roles and other identity-enhancing activities. As a result, they leave the majority of their students at loose ends and vulnerable to the destructive pressures of the toxic social environment.

By contrast, small schools enhance affirmation and identity because they draw kids into participation and leadership, because they offer challenges that stimulate the development of competence, and because they monitor behavior more effectively. Small schools enhance identity. We must make our schools smaller.

Visiting the smallest public high school in Nassau County (outside New York City), the high school from which I graduated three decades ago, I find even academically and socially marginal kids have a sense of belonging there. Kids say, "It's like a family here. You know you can count on everyone. You know everyone." They say, "You can't get away with anything here. Someone always notices what you are doing." That's a good recipe for competence and pro-social behavior and identity and affirmation: act so that the child will think, "People care about me, and they prove it by paying attention to what I do—both the good and the bad."

In my former school, at least, the influences of the environment were reduced by the school's functioning as a support system to enhance identity and pro-social behavior. The kids are not just coping with the socially toxic society. They are *thriving*. Other schools, however, are having the opposite effect.

The high school is the principal community institution in the lives of American teenagers. It is where they spend many of their days. It is where they work out the central issues of adolescence: forming an identity, negotiating peer relations, and preparing for adulthood. What happens here is important, for all of us. Thus, if we find social toxicity increasing in our high schools, it is cause for major concern. And concerned is what we should be.

The study of school size in the United States has an ironic history. Most of the important work was done in the 1950s and 1960s, and it documented the superiority of small schools in providing positive environments for teenagers. However, just as this evidence was becoming available, social forces and deliberate policy were closing and consolidating small schools in favor of intentionally big ones.

Put most simply, the research indicated that large schools tend to discourage teenagers from meaningful participation in the social and extracurricular activities of the school and diminish teenagers' sense of responsibility, especially if they are struggling academically. This is a particular problem because social and extracurricular activities are crucial to peer relations, and the direction a child's peer relations take does much to motivate that child's academic and vocational development in school. Extracurricular activities can support and enhance the academic agenda of the school if they bond students to the school and motivate them to behave responsibly. They can permit a wide variety of students to succeed and, therefore, encourage those students to develop a sense of involvement in, responsibility for, and commitment to the school. In today's world, this is especially important, since so many other aspects of life for teenagers are in turmoil. Faced with divorcing parents, uncertain economic prospects, violent television and movies, and the drug scene, teenagers *need* a solid school experience.

Researchers studying schools of varying sizes[9] reported that although the larger schools provide more settings in which students can act, there are proportionately more people to fill those settings (thus, schools are *overmanned*). Small high schools, by contrast, have more settings than people to fill them (thus they are *undermanned*). For example, although the large school may have both a chorus and a glee club, the two can accommodate only a very small proportion of the student body, so it is still hard for a given student to get into either activity. A small high school probably has just one vocal group, but that group is apt to be so hungry for voices that any student willing to make the effort will be welcomed.

Having attended a small high school as a teenager, I can attest to this myself. Rarely did anyone at that school have to try out for activities. It was mostly a case of showing up and demonstrating interest. In some cases, teachers and coaches went out of their way to recruit students to participate. They did this not because they were trying to be nice to students, but because they needed every possible student to make the activities work. The net result was high levels of participation; virtually everyone did something.

Of course, our football team did lose most of its games to bigger schools. But what is the point of high school sports, winning or participation? Unfortunately, I know the answer that many would give in a society that lionized Vince Lombardi's so-called ethic: "Winning isn't the most important thing, it's the *only* thing." The "winning is everything" ethic is a poison in a large school that can afford to be selective in deciding who gets to participate. It makes the school toxic for everyone, winners *and* losers.

The kinds of satisfactions differ in small schools as opposed to large ones. The researchers found that students from small schools reported satisfactions clustering around the development of responsibility, competence, challenge, and a sense of identity. That makes sense. They were being drawn into positions of responsibility and activity on behalf of pro-social goals—putting on concerts, organizing meetings, practicing and working in teams in preparation for competing in athletic events. This is the stuff of which healthy environments are made.

In contrast, most students in large high schools emphasized vicarious enjoyment, being part of a large crowd, watching the elite perform, and generally feeling part of a nameless, faceless crowd—what Barker and Gump called the "herd feeling."[10] It stands to reason that these kids would feel less active responsibility for the school and less sense of personal empowerment in their lives, and be less practiced in pro-social behavior. This would be a frightening combination of feelings in any time and place, but in a society such as ours, which is struggling with larger issues of social toxicity, it can be devastating to a child's psychological and social development. It can also be very costly to the whole community, fueling the problems of drug and alcohol abuse, alienation, and delinquency.

Not surprisingly, but very importantly, school-size effects are particularly prominent in the lives of marginal—academically struggling—students in large schools: those who come from low socioeconomic backgrounds, have difficulty academically, score lower on IQ tests, and have no family tradition of educational attainment. Large schools discriminate against marginal students because they can afford to do so. In large schools, marginal students are superfluous; in small schools, they are needed. It is not that teachers, coaches, and student leaders are more inclusive in small schools while those in large schools are elitist. It is a function of the situation itself, a socially toxic situation versus a socially healthy situation, and once again it is the most vulnerable kids who are at greatest risk.

I remember clearly that in my own high school each year there was a competition among the freshmen, sophomores, juniors, and seniors. We called it "Rock Rivalry." At stake was pride. The genius of the competition was that there were so many events that everyone in our small school was needed to complete all the tasks—build the refreshment stand; design and paint the posters and the mural; play on the volleyball, table tennis, and basketball teams; yell on the cheerleading squad; and produce the play—a full-fledged thirty-minute theater production (usually a musical comedy). The class leaders needed everyone, no matter how marginal.

Similarly, it was not uncommon for the football coach to prowl the halls in the fall actively recruiting any boy with two arms and legs who appeared to offer even the faintest athletic potential. I myself was one example. Contrast this with a large high school, where it is necessary to try out for every sport, every musical group, every group of any kind, and there are always more losers than winners.

It is not surprising that struggling students in small schools were more active than their large-school counterparts, and developed a stronger sense of responsibility toward the school and its activities. Psychologists recognize that people tend to become what their environment elicits and rewards, under the principle of progressive conformity discussed earlier. The big school elicits and rewards passivity and marginal involvement among most students, and leadership and activity only among the elite. The small school elicits and rewards participation and responsibility among the whole student body as a matter of necessity. Again, the big school is a more socially toxic environment for teenagers than the small school.

The real question is what constitutes "big" and "small" when it comes to high school size? Researchers of the 1950s and 1960s set out to define these terms, and their conclusion is disturbing but very relevant for understanding trends in social toxicity. After a school exceeded five hundred students for grades 9–12, the insidious social dynamics of bigness quickly came into play.[11]

It is clear that American high schools have become too big. From 1955 to 1975, the average size of American high schools increased from five hundred to fifteen hundred students and stayed there. Some of this was the result of deliberate policies that sought to increase the academic power of the schools, that sought fiscal savings in consolidation, and that favored the athletic power that tends to come with a large student body. Some of the growth resulted from communities adapting to the enormous increase in the size of the adolescent population as the post–World War II Baby Boomers grew into adolescence. Whatever the reasons in each specific case, the result was that more and more kids have been exposed to this form of social toxicity in the decades since the 1950s and 1960s.

The increase in school size took place at the same time our society was trying to reduce dropout rates and to get a higher percentage of kids through school to graduation. This is painfully ironic, because big schools are associated with *higher* dropout rates (presumably through their particularly pernicious effects on academically marginal students). As I see it, as the academic problems of students increase, ideal school size decreases, and yet our history has taken a very different turn: school size increased at the very time when more and more academically struggling students were being told to stay in school. What is more, big schools compound the problem of social class segregation by separating rich and poor into academically segregated tracks.

This is a telling observation when we think of the current problems—school crime, high dropout rates—among academically struggling students clustered in large high schools, when we think about the fortune being spent for security guards and metal detectors in schools, and when we think about the enormous amounts being spent to cope with vandalism and graffiti in schools. In 1986, one in five high school students nationwide reported fearing attack while in school, 13 percent reported carrying a weapon, and 8 percent were involved in a fight.[12] Just walk into a large high school and you will understand what I mean when I speak of a socially toxic environment. In contrast, walk into a small high school—if you can find one—and appreciate what a healthy social environment feels like. I did this as part of my thirtieth high school reunion (in 1994) and it was a wonderful experience. There is no graffiti. There are no security guards. There is no look of the war zone despite the presence of many at-risk youth and marginal students.

Small high schools provide an illuminating case study of how the processes of identity formation are linked to community, both in the sense of the school *as* a community and the school as a reflection of the larger community. The future is on the line with each group of children making the transition from childhood to adolescence. In a socially toxic environment we need to seize every positive opportunity we can to help kids make it through.

What Can We Do?

The first and most direct thing that parents can do to help their children build positive identities is to help them reclaim their time from the television. Watching TV may be easier for both parents and children than finding productive mutual activities, but life in that drugged sleep does neither parents nor children any good.

As parents and educators, we can work to find and provide appropriate—that is, small—sized schools for our children of all ages, and particularly for our adolescents. So long as we continue to put our kids in big schools, we are squandering the chance to provide positive opportunities for the kids who need them most. And we pay the price each time a marginal kid goes bad for lack of a positive experience of being needed, wanted, and affirmed.

But identity is more than just talents, skills, and artistic, athletic, and academic accomplishments. It is also a matter of character, of ethics, and of spirit. As parents, we must resist any "lowest common denominator" thinking about morality and behavior. Whether it's tolerating obscene language or caving in to buying the latest fad toy, it's not enough to justify behavior on the grounds that "everyone is doing it." No. If we expect leadership from our children we must exercise it ourselves. Only in this way can we help them become robust enough in their positive identities to avoid succumbing to the social toxicity that is all around them—and perhaps they will even help clean up that toxicity.

Chapter Six

Time Together

Making Human Beings Human

What do any of us really have, after all is said and done? We have our time on this earth (and whatever else our spiritual beliefs tell us may come before or after). When it comes to everything else, we are all just renting—or perhaps leasing. We *spend* our time. We *invest* our time. We *waste* our time. The clock ticks. What we do with our time is the single most important indicator of our values and beliefs about the world. We spend our time in all kinds of ways and must decide if we are spending it wisely or foolishly. Are we investing or wasting? When we spend time in preparation for some goal in the future, we are investing time with the expectation of payoff. The one thing we can't really do with time is save it: each moment passes and can never be recovered.

The Economy of Time

Economists try to capture childrearing and educational practices as aspects of human capital investment, and one of the ways we can invest time is in increasing human capital. Parents and teachers are investing time and energy to improve the quality of their products, whom we know as the children in their families and classrooms. This educational investment is crucial to the process of converting a human organism into a human being.

One of the powerful forces motivating business and government leaders to take a good hard look at childhood in our society in recent years has been growing concern about the product quality of our families and schools. When all is said and done, that quality boils down to the amount and quality of time invested. And what defines the quality of the time is the degree to which the people responsible for childrearing are committed to the task, and how well they know what they are doing. They also have to have the right raw materials—that is, children who are intellectually, emotionally, morally, and philosophically ready to learn—if their time is to be well used.

The economy of time is very important in childhood and in childrearing. How will children spend their time? Will they invest it in education or waste it in mindless television? Will they spend it with adults or with their peers? Every decision has implications for the well-being of children and the quality of the social environment. Every decision has an impact on human capital, now and in the future. Therefore, every decision is tied to the problem of social toxicity. If children invest their time in reading and doing their homework, the whole society benefits. If children instead spend their time cruising shopping malls and listening to pop music, we all suffer through lost productivity. The same goes for parents: the more time they spend in positive activities with kids the better their family's product will be—and the less, the worse.

What are our criteria for making decisions about spending, investing, or wasting time? One is what makes us happy. Another is the cost of alternatives. Time spent in one way is unavailable for use in another. What's it going to be, an hour spent playing ball with your children or an hour spent watching television? But why not both? Of course, this is a possibility in some situations. Some people have lots of time and few demands upon that time. They are time-rich, they can do everything they wish. However, for most of us, a large proportion of our time as individuals and as families is out of our control, making us time-poor rather than time-rich.

Time as Wealth

What determines whether or not you are time-rich? Many things contribute, but among the most important are your economic commitments. These commitments can be part of either the monetarized or the nonmonetarized economy. I'll describe our two economies in detail in Chapter Eight, but the basic concept is important here: value is value, whether it's exchanged for cash or not. If one child swims free in a clean lake, another pays a fee to swim in a city pool, and a third swims in a backyard pool that cost thousands of dollars, they *all* swim—and it is by no means clear that the alternative costing the most money conveys the greatest value. Many goods and services, especially those relating to family life and child care, are part of the nonmonetarized economy; people do them because they need to get done, without expecting to get paid in money. It is important for us to understand this concept and its implications because the nonmonetarized economy is rapidly becoming monetarized. The shift is having a radical effect on our values and particularly on the value we give to our time.

The minute something is transferred into the monetarized economy, it becomes subject to the calculations of cost effectiveness. When this happens, a whole new set of actors are drawn into the decision making about what we do and with whom. These new actors have financial profit as their goal. They are not necessarily bound to the larger purposes human activities can serve when they occur in the nonmonetarized economy. Investors in health care systems are looking for profit, not health care. Commercial theme park developers are interested in making money first and foremost, not in kids having fun. Video game promoters are interested in customers who have spending money, not children with interests. Of course it is possible for commercial enterprises to do good and still do well, but doing good is secondary to financial results in the monetarized economy. It must be, or the systems go bankrupt. The nonmonetarized economy is not necessarily more altruistic, but it does accept a much wider range of currencies: love, duty, religious belief, political ideology, barter, and good old-fashioned neighborliness.

These processes are at work in the matter of child care. How did we afford it in the past? "We" could afford it because women paid for it with their time and energy in the nonmonetarized economy—while men subsidized that time and energy through the cash income they derived from their participation in the monetarized economy.

Now we are trying to operate child care in the monetarized economy. We do this directly through paid child care and indirectly by expecting increasing numbers of people somehow to hold full-time jobs in both the monetarized and nonmonetarized economies. As a result, we are now coming to realize just how precious and expensive high-quality child care really is. Moreover, as child care appears in the GNP in a big way, there are for-profit entrepreneurs and corporations seeking to make money on it (and often cutting corners to do so). An observer of this scenario once told a colleague of mine, "You can't pay someone enough for what a parent will do for free." That's close enough to the truth to be useful as a guideline. Of course, parenting isn't free. Parents expect rewards. But their rewards come mostly in the nonmonetarized economy, and earning those rewards costs them plenty. Everyone who is a parent knows it takes time, energy, and sacrifice to do it right.

Although many with an economically conventional bent would argue that monetarizing child care is economic growth, others would argue that it reflects a net loss of care to many children and parents because of problems in funding high-quality care. This is a special kind of inflation, one not easily incorporated into the conventional economic thinking that dominates public policy. When governments look at the shift of child care from the nonmonetarized into the monetarized economy, they are just as likely to see this form of inflation as genuine economic growth.

Being Time-Poor or Time-Rich

In many technologically primitive societies, people spend most of their time meeting basic needs through the nonmonetarized economy. In Sudan, I met rural women who spent eight hours each day getting water and wood for cooking. They had long walks to and from the stream and the woodpile. Imagine how time-rich they felt when an international development agency put a well with a hand-operated pump in their village and showed them how to make energy-efficient stoves that cut their fuel use in half! They now had hours and hours of time freed up for other activities.

However, in our technologically modern societies, many of us are becoming as time-poor as those rural Sudanese women ever were. For us, the challenges come from the time-costly activities associated with working in the monetarized economy. Commuting to work, for example, is very costly, with hours per day not unusual in some places and for some workers, both urban and rural.

If we use the family rather than the individual as the unit whose time resources we measure, some clear themes emerge when we look back over the past forty to fifty years. Families now are much more time-poor than they once were. Families used to take care of their business during the work week. They earned their money 9 to 5, Monday to Friday. They also cleaned, shopped, cooked, took the kids to dentists and doctors, had repairmen in, and dealt with all the other aspects of running a household during that same period. Most stores and services were closed evenings and Sundays, and many were open only half a day on Saturdays. How could families take care of family business? They committed one adult primarily to the monetarized economy, Monday to Friday, 9 to 5, and committed the second adult to the nonmonetarized economy during that same period. As a result, families were time-rich. Evenings and weekends were free. In 1960, more than 60 percent of marriages had one parent in the monetarized economy and the other in the nonmonetarized economy. By 1990, that figure had dropped to less than 25 percent. And remember that the proportion of families with two adults has decreased also—from about 90 percent in 1960 to 70 percent in 1990.[1]

In addition to being time-poor, we have become more aware of opportunity costs. An *opportunity cost* arises when alternative uses of time compete, when doing A means you can't do B and when one of the two generates cash. If your son or daughter has a ball game Thursday night and your boss wants you to work that evening, you must choose. Attending the game costs the amount you would earn for those hours at work. Staying home to care for a young child costs you the salary you forego by doing so. Of course, opportunity costs increase as the market value of your time increases. It is a complicated chain of connection, but an important one. It costs a person earning $50.00 per hour twice as much in opportunity costs to attend a Little League game as it does someone earning $25.00 per hour and five times as much as it does a person earning $10.00 per hour.

With women on average now earning less than three-quarters of what men earn, it's pretty clear that if we think only about the financial costs and benefits then most families will end up with women spending more time with children than men—staying home with infants and sick children, working part-time to accommodate school schedules, and attending parent-teacher conferences. This remains true despite the massive increase in mothers working in the monetarized economy over the last forty years. In 1950, 22 percent of women with children were in the monetarized labor force (19 percent of those with preschoolers and 33 percent of those with older children). By 1990, that figure had risen to 67 percent overall (and 58 percent of mothers with preschoolers).[2]

Who is paying for this shift in the economic roles of mothers? The data tell us that fathers have not changed much. Mothers, in contrast, have typically made heroic efforts to keep up their productive activities in the nonmonetarized economy while stepping into the monetarized labor force. But there are limits to what even a mother can do or wants to do. Some fathers are stepping up their involvement, and some community institutions are increasing their efforts to help families adjust (as with after-school care programs).

Earning more money is always tempting, in part because it is easy to miss the price of that earning in time and energy that could be devoted to other activities. Few of us are immune to the financial payoffs in the monetarized economy, just we find it difficult to appreciate the costs in the nonmonetarized. And sometimes, rather than absorbing the nonmonetarized costs, we quietly expect someone else to incur them—which adds to the social toxicity of the environment.

Passing the Buck

To borrow a concept from studies of the physical environment, economists use the term *externalizing* to refer to the process of shifting costs on to someone beyond the scope of your responsibility. For example, consider a manufacturing process generating a stream of sludge that would cost $2,500 a day to process and dispose of safely. If the untreated sludge goes into a nearby river, the disposal is free as far as the factory owner is concerned, but the people downriver have to pay the cost of coping with polluted water. The factory has externalized its waste control costs. Obviously, the more you can externalize costs, the higher your profits will be—so long as the community you depend upon for employees, markets, and services continues to function despite the costs you are passing along to it. But it is very much in the community's interest to provide incentives for internalizing costs, and there are some incentives in place now. Bad publicity is one. Moral scruple is another. Public regulation is a third. Each does something to help. But the impulse to externalize remains strong nonetheless. In 1994, Congress debated (and ultimately rejected) measures designed to reduce externalization of costs for mining companies who use public lands for free (and thus reduce their out-of-pocket costs). The mining industry defeated attempts to make them internalize costs by paying a fee or royalty for their use of the land.

How does the concept of externalizing costs apply to child care in specific and families in general? For one thing, when employers do not assume responsibility for the physical and psychological effects of the workplace on employees, they are externalizing those costs. When families don't meet their responsibilities to care for their children, they are passing along those costs—externalizing them—to the larger community. The result: serious threats to human capital.

When we analyze human capital costs and benefits, we can take the viewpoint of the individual, the family, or the community. We come up with different costs and benefits for the same choices when we compare these three different viewpoints. For example, adolescents love to make money, but the ones who work in the monetarized economy more than twenty hours a week seem to suffer substantial costs in the nonmonetarized economy: their grades are lower, their investment in pro-social activities decreases, and their experimentation with drugs, alcohol, and sex increases.[3]

That's costly for the community, even though it puts more money in teenagers' pockets (and increases the GNP). Some families even depend upon teenagers' income to make ends meet. What adolescents choose to do with their earnings also has varying costs and benefits. If they use their money for immediate spending, they support the large consumer market that has grown up around teenagers' income. If they save it for college or some other future activity that will develop their abilities, they will make society more productive and satisfying. Their choice may also relate to their self-esteem—do they come to value themselves as consumers or as doers?

Similarly, families may increase their cash income by entering both parents in the monetarized workforce, but suffer substantial costs in the nonmonetarized world of the household—and feel stressed and guilty about those costs. At the same time, the community may be called upon to pick up the cost of child care. As the process of monetarization proceeds, opportunity costs and the impulse to shift costs to someone else rise proportionately. You do not face any opportunity costs if no one is offering to pay you for your time. If you do face opportunity costs, paying them may seem less attractive if your society denigrates the goods and services you might generate in the nonmonetarized economy. In a society where monetarization is widespread, the best things in life aren't free anymore. They are very costly—be those costs directly financial (as in the case of paying the admission price to the pool) or indirectly financial (as in the case of income lost through taking time off to go swimming).

Children thrive when adults invest time in them and spend time with them. Both are important. When the opportunity costs of family activities and the impulse to externalize them to someone beyond the family increase, as they have in our society over the last half century, the danger of social toxicity grows. The results are evident in ways that affect schooling, family life, and community institutions. Teachers today are unanimous in believing that parents expect the schools to do some of the basic socialization and caregiving for kids that used to take place at home. They don't say, "Parents are externalizing the costs of childrearing," but that's what they mean. The result, intended or not, is a growing unwillingness in our society to subsidize childhood as a time of freedom—free play, free feeling . . . free ride. This is evident in the increasing financial problems faced by schools. Tightening budgets put pressure first and foremost upon the key socializing aspects of education—extracurricular activities, meal programs, arts, and other nonclassroom activities.

Are Our Children Leaving Childhood Behind?

Every time I speak to a group of middle-class parents and professionals, the issue of "hurrying" comes up in the question period. The day I sat down to write the first draft of this page, I had spoken to the American Medical Association Alliance—a group composed primarily of physicians' spouses. After I finished, I was surrounded by members of the audience who wished to follow up with questions or comments. Among them was a woman who asked, "What about all the children who are so scheduled into lessons and other activities that they never have a chance to just play?" Her question is one that I see as being emblematic of our times (at least for affluent families). One source of social toxicity for children lies in the increasing demands for premature maturity. These demands set in motion a whole series of experiences for children that produce much pseudosophistication but little genuine social competence.

When my own son was eight, I knew that he wanted to be friends with the little girl who lived next door to us. But I never saw him playing with her. One day I asked him outright, "Why don't you just go over and play with her?" His response was sobering. "There's no room in her schedule!" he replied, and then began listing her daily regime of activities. He was right. She was all booked up.

Why are children all booked up at such a young age? Perhaps we can explain it with our economic model of families. When affluent parents see their children as an investment, the result is often greater and greater pressure on the children to yield dividends as measured by admission to competitive schools and display of precocious talents. In addition, those parents are so immersed in the monetarized economy that they can't afford to spend much time with their children or don't think they are expert enough to fine-tune their children's behavior and development, so they throw money at the problem instead. This leads to more pressure. Many families are spending unprecedented amounts of money on their children, and they want to see a return on their investment.

Gail Stout observes that "with computers and violins, swimming pools and gyms, today's baby-boom parents are determined to help their children be the best they can be."[4] Lessons and equipment (including computers) are major items in many family budgets. A recent comparison of children from the mid 1970s to late 1980s concluded that there had been a significant increase in children participating in sports, which I take to mean organized sports.[5] Others report that the massive proliferation of organized sports and recreation for children has not been matched by research to determine what, if any, effect organized activities have on speeding up the process of growing up or in altering the experience of play.[6]

We have to wonder whether kids really learn more in organized sports. Do they have more fun? Of course, it depends in part on the attitudes and behaviors of coaches and parents, but some who have observed the process at work believe that this drive to greater and ever-earlier payoffs increases the pressure on children to perform, to mature, and to succeed in ways that lend prestige to parents.[7] For example, for many families, success in school is of unprecedented importance. In the 1950s, high school graduation was an acceptable goal for middle-class kids, and there was no powerful stigma attached to dropping out before graduation for blue-collar kids. Now the expectations for educational attainment are much higher, and parents react to their fear that their children will be shut out of the economy by stepping up their efforts to obtain a competitive advantage. And while we can be concerned over the results they get, the real problem is not parental ambitions so much as it is a society under siege.

Parents and educators raise their academic expectations for young children in anticipation of future competition. Many teachers and parents expect children to be reading as they enter first grade, and often express the concern that children who are not reading fluently by Christmas are delayed and perhaps even possess a learning disability. Secondary school graduation has come to be defined as a prerequisite for full personhood in U.S. society. For the affluent, a college education is imperative. All this means that children are under greater pressure to pay off in academic skills than ever before. In this climate, free play may seem a luxury children cannot afford if they are to be successful—even though there are good reasons to believe that free play is the best investment for later life success. The competition among affluent families of young children for academic success sometimes appears to have the intensity observed among elite Japanese families, who use the term *Mama-gom* (monster mother) to describe this pressure-cooker environment.[8]

This is not totally new, of course. Survey evidence from an affluent suburban community collected by CBS News in the mid 1960s and presented in a film report entitled "16 in Webster Groves" revealed a high level of academic competition and stress among college-bound secondary students. What is new, it seems, is the widespread lowering of the age for this pressure and its spread to more and more families. Then it was in high school; now it is in elementary school. That's a significant change, because it means childhood is being invaded.

While affluent children face demands that they mature rapidly in academic work, children across the socioeconomic spectrum face demands that they mature rapidly in social behavior. The profound changes in family structure and stability that have come upon us over the last few decades place heavy social demands on children. Many single parents look to their children as confidantes, as friends, and as advisers. Divorce and dating or remarriage by parents demand interpersonal sophistication on the part of children at an early age. Part of this is unintentional sexualization. It is hard enough for most kids to accept the idea that their parents are sexual beings at all. It is still harder for them to deal with the thought that "this man is not my father and he's sleeping with my mother!"

Most divorced parents of young children remarry, so most children of divorce experience maternal and paternal courtship. The glorification of a "sophisticated" lifestyle in the mass media (dressing fashionably and being sexually provocative, for example) goes hand-in-hand with greater demands for children to act mature. The demands on children are evident if you sit in on one of the divorce support groups found in many schools, particularly those serving affluent populations. Despite cute names like "Banana Splits," these groups testify to the superficial sophistication (and the real sense of loss) many children develop when exposed to the dissolution of a marriage: the kids look grown up and talk grown up, but they are often hung up on resolving some basic issues of childhood such as attachment.

Research on the impact of divorce on kids reveals a pattern of significant but small effects on standard measures of psychological functioning in children. What these measures often do not capture is the long-term, perhaps permanent pain that kids feel when families split up. I was talking about this research with a colleague at a reception recently. Her parents' divorce was a decade ago, and she is now a married woman herself, and yet her eyes misted over with tears as she recalled (and thus relived) the pain that she felt. She is not unique, or even unusual for that matter. Few people divorce casually. Nonetheless, most spouses are not fully prepared for the pain suffered all around.

One result of the trend toward less stable families appears to be that children have a greater sense of appreciation for the contingent nature of parental involvement. Parents are not forever, and even when marriages remain intact, children often must compete with work and other activities for parental time and attention. The fifty-year follow-up to the classic Middletown community study sheds some light on the situation.[9] The investigators repeated questions posed to teenagers about their parents more than half a century ago. In 1924, 63 percent of the adolescents reported that the most desirable attribute of a father is the fact that he spends time with his children. Only 38 percent placed a premium on mothers who spent time with their children. Does this mean kids in 1924 didn't value their mothers as much as their fathers? Not really. What it means is that they took their mothers for granted. When I was growing up, my mother showed her awareness of this by saying such things as, "That's right, leave your clothes around. Old Slobbo will pick them up!" On the other hand, kids appreciated that fathers who spent time with them were doing something special. By 1977, however, things had changed. Sixty-two percent of kids said the most valuable thing about a mother is that she spends time with them (and 68 percent said the same of fathers).

These data suggest that maternal involvement has become more valued, but they also suggest that children recognize they can't count on their mothers to be available to them any more than they can their fathers. It is important for both parents to be valued, so it can be argued that these children have a useful insight that their predecessors lacked. However, it still ought to be possible to find ways to offer children the basic reassurance of commitment that they need. To understand this, we must address another issue, the pressure on children to replace adult supervision with self-supervision in response to changing roles for mothers and the intransigence of fathers and the larger community. Many of our children seem to be hearing the message "Hurry up and grow up."

The Changing Role of Women and the Unchanging Role of Men

Most women today, even if they are mothers, want to be part of the monetarized labor force. They find it conveys a sense of worth and accomplishment. This is an inevitable by-product of the increasingly monetarized nature of our society (and it helps explain why teenagers want to earn money too).

In 1970, 53 percent of the women polled by a *New York Times* survey named "being a mother and raising a family" and 43 percent named "being a homemaker," as one of the two or three "most enjoyable things about being a woman today." The comparable figures for 1983 were 26 percent and 8 percent. "Career, jobs, pay" and "general rights and freedoms" increased from 9 percent to 28 percent and from 14 percent to 32 percent, respectively. It worries me to consider the implications of this trend for the 1990s, let alone for the next century.

Beyond wanting the satisfaction that a paycheck brings, many women face basic financial pressures that force them to work in the monetarized economy. Families need income-generating mothers, whether it be for affluence (two middle-class workers), protection from low income (two blue-collar workers), or sheer survival (a single parent). Two incomes lift middle-class families into the affluent range and prevent low-income families from slipping into poverty.[10]

The demand for getting the most out of parental money-making capacity is leading us to a crisis in child care and supervision. Who takes care of the children while the parents are out making money? In early childhood, the answer is day care or some other alternative care arrangement. But during the elementary school years, the pressure grows to move the responsibility for child care onto the shoulders of the child. Parents try to cope with demands of the world of work and the high cost of child care by enlisting children to care for themselves. Necessity is the mother of invention, to be sure. But necessity may also give rise to rationalization.

Is it good for kids to take care of themselves before they enter adolescence? Children who start in self-care at ages eight or nine are twice as likely as children with adult care to be experimenting with drugs, alcohol, and sex by the time they are fifteen years old.[11] Why? Because they live in a socially toxic environment. In this environment, if children are to make a go of it, they need more rather than less adult supervision, more rather than less intensive socialization to reduce susceptibility to negative peer influences, to mass media influences, to the low self-esteem produced by the big school, and more rather than less connection with their parents. And yet the modern economy and parental roles in that economy stimulate and reinforce rationalizations like the following: "Children don't need adults, they need to be free," and "Children can cope with a lot more than we give them credit for," and "Children understand that their parents have to live their own lives too," and "The sooner children grow up the better off they will be in the long run."

In our current culture, parents have a strong incentive to believe that young children are capable of assuming early responsibility for self-care and that early demands for maturity are in the child's best interest. And they are likely to make more and more decisions based not upon what the child needs but what the child can tolerate. This process of rationalization leads inevitably to the implication that there is something wrong with children if they cannot meet the demands placed upon them by adults who are responding to the demands placed on them. And so on and so on. Where and when this family trend to give the child increasing responsibility takes place in a safe, secure, and supportive environment, it may proceed without major and obvious consequences. But that is not the society we live in. The changes in levels of adult supervision of children within the family are taking place in the context of an environment that is more and more socially toxic for children.

Don't Parents Care About Their Children?

Visiting a third-grade classroom in a middle-class suburb, I asked, "How many of you have a grown-up there when you go home after school?" About a third shook their heads and kept their hands down. That's about average for eight-year-olds today; in some places, the figure is higher, even for younger children. By the time kids are nine, a majority are home alone. Some call these kids *latchkey children*. Others prefer the term *children in self-care*. Whatever you call them, they are a product of the U.S. economy, an economy that draws parents into the workplace to make a living in a society that assigns personal value on the basis of financial productivity.

Many parents believe they have few alternatives. Women need to work in the cash economy. Despite evidence of some shift in traditional orientations to role division,[12] few men are ready, willing, and able to alter traditional patterns that define child care as the mother's responsibility regardless of her labor force participation.[13]

The problem generally lies with separated or divorced fathers who fail to provide child support payments, and thus force mothers to give up time with their children in order to be able to feed them. It lies with fathers who live with their children but don't assume full responsibility for day-to-day care. It lies with unaccommodating workplace managers or unsympathetic policy makers.

The issue is acute with respect to infants and preschool children who are in full-time day care. Their parents do not have, or at least do not believe they can afford, the luxury of giving the child and themselves the choice of being at home where developmentally enhancing free play can flourish. Even when poverty is not the issue, most families are so hooked on the amenities of modern monetarized life that they truly believe they cannot manage without them. Thus, they need as much income as they can possibly generate.

They need the child to enter the most inexpensive care, even though that care probably involves regimentation and attention to group needs that suppresses developmentally enhancing free play. This type of pressure is particularly often found in profit-oriented centers.[14] Families trying to maximize cash income need the child to manage well in care. They need the child to attend school or be in the day-care setting as much as possible. Children may feel (or be) pressured to keep attending after they become sick, or start attending again before they are well, to make things work better for their parents.

Conventional economic thinking does not fully consider the true costs of caring for children. There are limits to the number of children that one caregiver can serve without compromising development. This is one reason why large family size is a risk factor in development—parents do not have enough time to go around. The same is true for day care. Staff-child ratios must be kept low to protect the development process; however, given the limited financial resources of the families they serve, family day care providers who serve less-than-affluent families usually cannot generate sufficient income per child to set a proper limit on the number of children in their care. An analysis conducted in Illinois illustrated this problem.[15]

Workers at the factory studied could afford to pay no more than $30 per week per child for care. A family day care provider who accepted four children—the approved number—could thus earn only $5,500 per year. Most responded by increasing the number of children cared for to eight and by seeking to stay outside the licensing system. The cost of this pattern of care is borne in decreased developmental prospects for the children. The same analysis concludes that it cost at least $55.00 per week per child to provide adequate care. The "missing" $25 contributes to the social toxicity of the environment for children. Why are these children exposed to these child care situations? Their families are struggling to meet the financial demands of the monetarized economy in which they live. As always, it is the most vulnerable members of the population who suffer most from growing up in a socially toxic environment.

Beverly Cleary writes books for young people. In those books, she developed a set of characters who exemplify the desirable essence of childhood. As the decades of her career have passed and she has taken note of the changing nature of family life, her characters have come to speak for and about the dynamics of contemporary demands for maturity. Her Huggins and Quimby families are archetypical middle-class American families, and it is thus significant that in a 1981 book, Ramona Quimby, Age 8, eight-year-old Ramona is beset by worry that if she gets sick at school it will interfere with her mother's work schedule. In a 1984 book, Ramona Forever, Ramona becomes a latchkey child. Ramona adapted to the 1980s.[16] In the 1990s, Ramona seems passé, so far have things gone for so many children and their families.

In a nation where everything costs money and continues to cost more, most families need two incomes to keep up—at the same time that divorce and single parenthood leave more and more families with only one potential wage earner. Most families used to have a buffer. If a child got sick, someone could be home. If the principal wage earner was laid off, the other adult could find a job to compensate. By holding one adult in reserve, families could spread themselves more evenly between the monetarized and nonmonetarized economies. They didn't have all their eggs in one basket.

Now they do. If they have two cash incomes, they probably need both to meet their commitments in the cash economy. If they don't have two incomes, chances are they only have one adult in the household, who must struggle to bring home a paycheck and take care of the many nonmonetarized activities that remain in the household economy—things like child care, health care, play, neighboring, homework, and so on.

When we look back over the last fifty years, we can see clearly that children are increasingly an economic burden, directly because of what it costs to raise them and indirectly because of what they cost in lost parental income, time away from the job that over a childhood comes to tens of thousands if not hundreds of thousands of dollars. The opportunity costs of childrearing create another element of social toxicity for children.

Very young children are expected to be ready to go into out-of-home child care arrangements as early as is humanly possible so that parents can get back to work. Children are left alone more and earlier so parents can stay at work because it costs so much to provide adult supervision. Children remain in school longer after they get sick and return to school sooner when they begin to get well because parents cannot afford to leave work to care for a sick child at home. All of this puts pressure on children; those who cannot manage see themselves as failures. All of it makes the environment for children more socially toxic.

What Can We Do?

Parents need to remind themselves that their rewards need not all be in the future, when they can be shown to have raised a successful child. Childrearing brings intense personal rewards for those who are there to enjoy watching their children develop. Few experiences rival the joy. Increasing time spent together provides incentives to pay the opportunity costs of childrearing, to make choices that benefit children. It can be counterproductive to exert too much pressure on children. It can decrease a child's security and stability to be pressured, and that can prove costly in later behavioral problems.

If you can't find a way to make your work time more flexible, then consider giving up your television time or your social time. Some employers are becoming more flexible about when and where employees do their work. If you do some work at home, you can spend former commute time with your children. Large employers can be encouraged to have day care on or near the premises or to contribute to day-care costs. Cafeteria-style benefit plans can offer help with day care as a benefits choice.

Highly skilled workers responsible for children can often get employers who need their services to agree to arrangements that fit into children's schedules. The same skills and attitudes that make their own investments in children pay off, pay off for the company that employs them. Some employers do this already, and more should be encouraged to do so.

But home and workplace schedule revisions won't do everything. We also need to start debating the issue of hurrying our children into faster maturity, and weighing its costs against the value of immediate cash income. Parent education may be a factor here. Both parents and educators should work to understand the benefits of middle-class childhood for the quality of life in our society. There is much that can be done once we all realize why it must be done.

Chapter Seven

Values and Community

Becoming Part of the Bigger Picture

What do we believe in? This is an important question for parents to answer. Our children ask it every day, sometimes in words, always in their silent observation of what we adults do and say. What do we believe in? How do we demonstrate our beliefs to our children? These are important questions because children need to feel a connection to something more than the injunction to "have a nice day." They need to be anchored in positive values—the more so, as they face our socially toxic environment.

The Value of Values

Each of us must examine what messages our lives are sending to our children about what matters and what doesn't. The modern world tends to erode belief. It substitutes the social conventions of fashion and cynicism for the enduring values of caring and spirituality. When Imelda Marcos was overthrown as the dragon lady of the Philippines, it was discovered that she possessed a thousand pairs of shoes. How did we react? Some reacted with envy, others with amusement. Few seemed to appreciate the obscenity of it. But just how many pairs of shoes are "moral" in a world in which billions are virtually shoeless? How many of us are on the right path?

Are shoes a moral issue? They are in a consumer culture, where everything is disposable and the only real criterion of value is quantity. What values are we teaching our children if we appear to endorse this culture to the exclusion of other values? Consumerism, and the universal disposability it entails, is surely one of the challenges to families in a socially toxic environment such as ours. Children find it hard to learn to value caring when they see disregard all around them. And they find it hard to learn to value responsibility when they see callous and gratuitous waste all around them. Some years ago, I was thinking of what could be the most ludicrous example I could find to illustrate the mentality of disposability. I hit upon the idea of the "Disposable Phone—Make One Call and Then Throw It Away." I thought this bit of hyperbole would make my point well. However, by the time my book was published, I was reading in the newspaper about hospitals and hotels offering disposable phones to their customers. The disposable mentality teaches lessons to children. At its extreme, we see children killed because someone wants their leather jacket not because the thief is coatless but because the new coat is "cool." The question is: are these the lessons we want the next generation to learn?

Those lessons reach every child, but they hit particularly hard with children living on the edge of society. The grossness of the drug-dealer lifestyle—hot cars, jewelry, flashy clothes, ostentation— is a revealing parody of mainstream consumerism, in which cars and clothes are valued as indicators of status.

Researchers report a 25 percent increase in childhood obesity in the United States over the last twenty-five years. It seems the problem lies with too many kids sitting around snacking while they watch television, instead of getting out and doing things.

Family Commitment

Recall from Chapter Three that particularly today, commitment is an essential element in successful families. When the family is important to its members, much energy and time are directed inward toward the family as a unit. Being a successful family today requires some hard choices. Many things compete for the time and energy of family members—work, school, friends, hobbies, recreation. In the modern world, you can't do everything. When there are no options, being committed to family is easy: it's the only show in town. But choosing family is often hard work when there are many attractive alternatives.

The commitment needed to sustain families today has to come from somewhere. The power to make and maintain it often springs from a religious or spiritual orientation, though it can also come from a secular belief system or ideology. The point is that families need to be connected to something larger than mere existence. Children and adults need a sense of purpose, a sense that their lives together mean something more than just getting up, eating, going to school or work, watching TV, and going to bed. This is a deep spiritual need, and meeting it strengthens the fabric of the family.

A strong family must explore and proclaim a life of values for children. For some, this will mean religious commitments and spirituality. For others, it will mean living a political life as a testament to the importance of translating community values into practice. This can mean volunteering on behalf of human rights advocacy groups, mobilizing neighbors to seek more effective local government, and participating in other efforts to increase social justice. For all of us, it can mean teaching our children through words and deeds that we care for the planet—through recycling and conservation, through efforts to protect habitats and the creatures who inhabit them, through taking responsibility for small pieces of the natural environment, through living lightly upon the earth.[1]

For Americans today, Green Consciousness can be a spiritual and political core to which children can relate with strength and enthusiasm. Save the dolphins—and save ourselves. . . . The bottom line is believing in something noble, and translating that belief into action that children can see and learn from. It means making connection with the infinite resources of the human spirit.

Moral Development

Some years ago, I visited with a ten-year-old Palestinian girl living in a refugee camp during the *Intifada*—the uprising against Israeli rule in the West Bank and Gaza. I asked her to explain to me how she dealt with fear when soldiers raided her home at night. "I reassure the younger kids," she told me. "How?" I asked. "I explain to them that the soldiers are people just like us," she said. "I tell them that the soldiers are acting under orders when they do things to us here. When they go home to their families they are good fathers to their children." Hearing this level of moral discourse from a child living under extreme threat was humbling and inspiring at the same time.

How did she acquire this moral framework for her life? Someone taught it to her. Someone moved her along from primitive to advanced moral thinking. Lev Vygotsky referred to this process of operating in the developmental space between what the child can do alone and what the child can do with the help of a teacher as the Zone of Proximal Development.[2] Developmentalists have come to recognize that it is the dynamic relationship between the child's competence alone and the child's competence in the company of a guiding teacher that leads to forward movement. And that's where my little friend learned her morality—from her father, a kind teacher who showed her the way.

This seems particularly important in moral development, in which the child's moral teachers (be they adults or peers) lead the child toward higher-order thinking by presenting positions that are one stage above the child's characteristic mode of responding to social events as moral issues.

When this cognitive process is coupled with a warm family, the result is ever-advancing moral development, and the development of a principled ethic of caring.[3] What is more, even if the parents block this process by treating the child in a rigid, authoritarian way, the larger community may compensate. Only a minority of adults ever achieve the highest levels of moral reasoning, but these adults can exert leadership beyond their numbers.

Thus, the issue of stimulating moral development is a social one. Adults in the community outside the family (most notably schoolteachers) must demonstrate the higher-order moral reasoning necessary to move children from the lower to the higher stages. In addition, these adults need to create a cadre of moral leaders among children and youth, young leaders who can set the moral tone for their peers. The failure of adults to take these roles contributes heavily to the development of a socially toxic environment. Without adult leadership, moral development tends to fall to the lowest common denominator rather than being uplifted to the highest possible standard.

Values at the Lowest Common Denominator

From my perspective, the most important consequence of leaving children to cope based on their own resources is the impact it has on their values. This problem is doubled and redoubled when children are aware of—or worse yet, exposed to—traumatic violence, as they are on a daily basis in our current environment. A socially toxic environment like ours generates juvenile vigilantism.

When children learn that they cannot rely upon adults to protect them, they are likely to turn to themselves and their peers. No kid wants to feel afraid, and any kid will try to do what it takes to change that situation. If it means joining a gang, so be it. If it means carrying a gun, so be it. If it means adopting a tough, nasty facade, so be it. Anything is better than being afraid all the time, particularly if that fear is accompanied by the social conditions that undermine self-worth—poverty, racism, abandonment.

Psychologists like Stephen Asher have studied the "legitimization of aggression" among elementary school children.[4] They find that the more kids agree with statements validating aggression—such as "It's OK to hit someone if they hurt your feelings" and "It's

OK to hit someone if they hurt you"—the more aggressive they are in the classroom, on the school yard, and in the neighborhood.

Unless we reach them with healing experiences and offer them a moral and political framework within which to process their experiences, traumatized kids are likely to be drawn to values and ideologies that legitimize and reward their aggression, their rage, their fear, and the hateful cynicism that they feed upon in our culture.

I think this is one reason why ideology is so important to the process of moral development, and coping more generally. If schoolteachers and other adult representatives of the community are disinclined to model higher-order moral reasoning or are intimidated if they try to do so, then the process of moral deterioration that is natural to stressful situations will proceed unimpeded. If the leaders of children's peer groups do not speak for higher values, then the quality of social life deteriorates. This is one of the ways in which the socially toxic environment develops its own negative momentum. It has happened in American communities. In some neighborhoods, the power of gangs seems irresistible and potential moral leaders are inhibited. In others, it is because it is not socially acceptable to speak up. In both cases it means trouble, particularly when the forces of social toxicity are gathered as they are today in America. If little kids are to stand tall so must the adults in their lives. Moral courage is one of the antidotes to social toxicity. I fear it is in short supply.

Community: Connecting to the World Outside the Home

Our profoundly individualistic culture has many attractions, but it also contributes very heavily to our toxic social environment. In order to detoxify that environment, one of the first steps we take must affirm this most fundamental of political principles: *parenthood is a social act*. As individual parents and as citizens, this is where we must start in our thinking. Children may be conceived by individual adults, but they live as social beings, inextricably tied to social forces and institutions. The individualistic culture of American life obscures this reality, and we all suffer as a result.

In 1985, my family moved to Illinois. We brought with us a three-year-old car, our Volkswagen, and a three-year-old child, our daughter. After we arrived, we soon received messages from the state: register your car; get your car inspected; get your car insured; get a license to operate your car. We got the message: Illinois cares about cars. But what about our daughter? Nothing. Not a word. She was officially invisible.

This experience illuminates the problem we all face in creating and sustaining supportive relationships between families and their communities, relationships that recognize the fundamental fact that parenthood is a social act. Every time a child is born in our society, it should start its life as a member of the community. Right now, it doesn't. This must change if anything else is to change.

A good place to start would be with universal home health visiting. Every pregnant woman should automatically be enrolled in a supportive relationship with a home health visitor. This relationship should continue at least for the first two years of the child's life, and it should include everything from basic health care to parent education and counseling as needed. Doing this would make a statement of social connection. It would acknowledge that children count in the community at least as much as cars.

Taking Responsibility for All Our Children

Earlier, I described how important it is for children to feel they have a family home. It is only a small step from this concept of home to the political idea of homeland, the sense that you are part of a nation, that you belong somewhere politically. I believe that both home and homeland are important in figuring out who you are, that is, in the formation of your identity. If you lack either or both, you are likely to suffer from problems of alienation, rootlessness, and depression. A family generally finds it hard to function well without a home, both in the narrow sense of having a permanent residence and in the larger sense of being part of an intact community.

This is one way to interpret Kai Erikson's study of families who lost both their homes and their community as the result of a devastating flood.[5] In *Everything in Its Path*, Erikson highlighted the psychological and social problems encountered by these families as they sought simultaneously to build new homes and a new community. They were depressed, irritable, angry, inclined to misuse alcohol, and generally had a hard time picking up the threads of their lives. His study directs our attention to the intense social toxicity that arises when whole communities become uprooted. For very young children, the principal danger is that a demolished community will demoralize their parents. For older children and for adolescents there is another danger, that the lack of community itself will prove harmful.

To understand the development of children in a socially toxic environment, we need to consider whether or not they are homeless in the larger sense of lack of community. More and more children and youth are growing up with a sense of rootlessness that comes from the double whammy of family disintegration coupled with a sense of homelessness in the larger society. When this happens, it is a failure of our society—of us all—as surely as it is a failure of the individual family unit.

Communities Need Economic Diversity

Economic character constitutes an important dimension of any community. The increasing geographic concentration of poverty in America is an important indicator of growing toxicity and a challenge to our belief in community. A study in Cleveland revealed that the percentage of that city's poor people living in neighborhoods with concentrated poverty (that is, more than 40 percent of the residents were poor) increased from 21 percent in 1970 to 61 percent in 1990).[6] This is not good news. Economically mixed areas offer more advantages to both the middle class and the poor. For the poor, the presence of multiple role models offers concrete alternative answers to the question, "How else might I live?" In addition, poor kids have potential access to families with extra resources that can be shared—an extra ticket to the ball game, a visit to the zoo, an inside look at what middle-class life is like and what it takes to move up. For affluent kids, living in proximity to poor families is a good antidote for negative stereotypes. Without rubbing shoulders with poor kids and having an opportunity to form authentic relationships, affluent kids must depend upon the news media, social studies classes, and chance encounters to give poverty a human face.

I suspect the growing estrangement of affluent and poor families is one reason why when an informal survey of middle-class children posed the following question, "Which would be worse, to be poor or to be blind?" a majority of the children chose "poor" as the worse alternative. Why? When asked to explain, one child replied that "you could do something about being blind, but you couldn't do anything about being poor."

Childish thinking? A distorted value system? Perhaps. But perhaps these children were on the mark in assessing the life implications of poverty in the United States today, where poverty is coming to be more and more intractable at both the personal and the social levels and an affluent person has many more resources than a poor person to turn to in dealing with life's troubles, including blindness. All this gets played out as a prime ingredient in a community's life and identity. But it is not simply mounting segregation of the poor that prevents children and adults from forming relationships across classes.

The Effects of Television

Television presents a world full of threat, and in particular it presents a threatening view of the way people from different classes treat each other. In general, the more television you watch, the more paranoid your view of the community around you. I discussed this once with a woman who manages a high-rise unit of housing for the elderly. "That explains a lot," she said. "The old people in my building do two things, sit in their rooms watching TV and come down to the lobby to talk about how scared they are to go out!" Old and young are the most vulnerable; they reveal the high level of social toxicity around us all.

And U.S. kids watch a lot of television—most of it adult television. It is not surprising that they come away from that experience with a sense that the world is a hostile and threatening place. The level of predatory behavior on television is very high: maniacs, killers, and thieves abound.

Researchers report that high dosages of television viewing result in increased social paranoia. That is, people who watch more TV have increased fear and distrust of the community. This reinforces the other major effect of television, which is to suppress social interaction in both the family and the community. A Canadian study revealed that after the introduction of television in a community, face-to-face interaction declined significantly (by about 25 percent).[7] Thus TV undermines community in the sense of people building relationships face to face, replacing it with a collective culture of broadcast images that predispose them to distrust each other.

A related problem today is isolation of children from their communities because of parental concern about the dangers to be found on the streets. For example, the parent who prohibits the child from playing outside for fear of kidnapping (a fear based on mass media reports) may be denying the child a chance to engage in social and athletic play and to come to know the sources of strength and support in the neighborhood. Thus, social isolation becomes an undesirable side effect of protecting the child from potential (although statistically remote) harm. What is more, the ongoing stress to everyone involved may take its toll through increased anxiety and decreased pleasure in the ebb and flow of community life—driving them to take refuge still more often before the television. Many communities are struggling with proposals to set curfews for teenagers. But the real issue is not getting the kids *off* the streets as much as it is getting the adults *on* the streets. It *feels* safer to have neighbors out and around, and it *is* safer because the informal systems of supervision are at work.

What Can We Do?

Emphasizing community is a profound challenge to the divisive forces at work in modern American culture. Many of us have become almost embarrassed to admit *having* values that go beyond politically correct platitudes, let alone acting on them, and we need to set that feeling aside. We need to accept as fact that beyond our roles as parents of our own children we have a role as citizens responsible for everyone's children. We need to set high standards for public behavior. Research demonstrates that teenagers who perceive community monitoring to be a fact of life (that is, who believe if they do something wrong in the community someone will notice and do something about it) are less likely to engage in negative behavior, including using drugs.

Families need to acknowledge and respond to their communities, but there are also things people should do to help their communities become positively involved with families, by promoting universal home health visiting and similar outreach programs. Campaigns like "Healthy Families America"—sponsored by the National Committee to Prevent Child Abuse—deserve general support, because they are important for our future as a society. We need to institutionalize an ethic of caring.

We can also demonstrate our care for our communities—and the way our communities care—by supporting community initiatives to increase recreational activities that provide constructive challenges for children and youth, letting them experience achievement. In addition to recreation, we should offer children and youth opportunities for community service, so that their identities include helping others as a concrete fact rather than a hollow admonition.

We can strive for communities that are diverse rather than choosing to live in enclaves where everyone is like us. And wherever we live, we can take an active approach to our communities, rather than huddling in our homes. We can turn off the TV (or at least watch programs *together* with our children and talk about what we have seen). We can also make more occasions for meeting and talking to people and include our children in these occasions.

We can become members of active community groups—joining people with like interests in clubs, civic organizations, and philanthropic organizations that teach important lessons by example. Basic family memberships at places like the city zoo, botanic gardens, art museum, historical museum, and library are generally not very expensive and offer regular admission as well as special family events like picnics and tours.

Besides providing a living lesson in practical values, active community participation can have the added benefit of helping defuse unwarranted fears of strangers. It puts pro-social adults on the streets to protect children and discourage predatory adults. It grounds the community in a child's experiences. This provides a basis for recognizing the real dangers that do exist without fostering paranoia. Helping children accomplish this complex balancing act is vitally important.

The idea of raising a child by yourself in isolation is unnatural to us as social animals; yet when the community takes the view that parents are, or should be, wholly responsible for their children, parents are isolated from the kinds of support that only a community can give. We need to identify the support parents might need and take community as well as individual responsibility for children. We need to value what community can accomplish and the caring it can create.

It would be unconscionable to talk about values and community activity without also addressing people's access to basic needs, or economic justice. Economic forces shape—and often misshape—community life. The evolution of our economic life over the last few decades has increased social stress on children, at both the top and the bottom of the economy. Our strategies for using economic resources on behalf of children have not kept pace with the size and complexity of our economy, and with the process of modernization. The middle-class family is truly the bedrock of U.S. society. Therefore, the growing erosion of the economic middle—more rich and more poor and fewer genuinely middle-class families—is one of the most insidious aspects of social toxicity, one that we *must* address. Chapter Eight takes up that part of the story.

Chapter Eight

Access to Basic Resources

Achieving Economic Justice

At present, about one in five U.S. children overall and two in five children six and under live below the officially defined poverty line. By historical and global standards this may seem a relatively small number, for in many countries of the world the figure is more like 65 percent. But when contrasted with the affluence of our society and the success of other modern societies in protecting children from poverty, the U.S. data represent a telling statistical accusation,[1] a story that increasingly affects *all* our communities, not just inner-city neighborhoods. No discussion of reforming the environment for children can be complete without addressing economic reformation, a reformation in our thinking as well as in our doing, a reformation that comes to terms with poverty and the increasing monetarization of our economy.

The Meaning of Poverty

What does it mean to be poor in the United States? In one sense, this question is easy to answer, and Sophie Tucker pointed us in the right direction when she said, "I've been rich and I've been poor . . . and rich is better." Good as they are, however, the question and the answer are insufficient. We need more.

When my mother was a child in England, she was poor. She recalls being sent by her mother to the local money lender to borrow enough to feed the family's children until Friday when her father got paid. Sixty years later, she still feels the shame of it. It was not the simplicity of the material conditions of her childhood that was the problem. It was the social threat, the *vulnerability*. Poverty is hardly ennobling, particularly in a society in which the contrasts between rich and poor are reinforced daily in the mass media.

During the 1960s, 32 percent of poor people in the United States moved out of poverty within a year of becoming poor; during the 1980s, only 23 percent experienced that same recovery.[2] Being poor becomes more and more a condition of life rather than an event in a family's history. In North America, families with young children are more likely to be poor than other segments of the population. That trend is especially problematic, and it is increasing. Poverty early in life is a special threat to development, at the most basic level because it can compromise a child's biological and psychological systems.

By official government policy, an objective definition of poverty exists. It is based upon the income needed to meet an agreed-upon minimal standard of living. Thus, the poverty line at a given time and place is defined as X dollars for a family of Y persons. But like most objective classifications of complex human phenomena, this simple definition conceals a host of subtleties and complexities of what poverty means for children.

Being poor means being at statistical risk. Surveys tell us that poor children live in the kinds of environments that generate such multiple threats to development as academic failure, maltreatment, and learning disabilities. That is one clear meaning of being poor in the United States. Being poor also exposes one to more physical toxicity as well. Low-income populations are more likely to be exposed to chemical and radioactive waste and polluted air and water. Being poor means that the statistical odds are stacked against you. However, it has other meanings as well.

The daughter of a colleague of mine once wrote in a composition for school that she was "the poorest kid on her block" because she lived in the smallest house. She did live in the smallest house on the block. However, it was a seven-bedroom house on a block of mansions. What does it mean to children to be poor if their standard is that being poor is having less than others?

When most people around the world live on incomes of a few hundred dollars a year, what does it mean to define the U.S. poverty level at $14,000 a year? India defines poverty as having access to less than 2,100 calories per day[3] and, using that yardstick, estimates 20 percent of the population are poor (a figure roughly the same as ours). If poor children around the world are shoeless, how do we make sense of U.S. poor kids wearing $150 running shoes? In China, a man once reported to me that before the 1948 revolution very few people were rich but now many people were rich. As evidence, he pointed to the fact that he himself owned a wristwatch, a radio, and a bicycle. By that standard, poverty is virtually absent in the United States, and we Americans are all rich.

Analyzing the meaning of poverty for children is not simple. It is not a matter of simple accounting. Rather, it calls for thinking about the relationship between the meaning and meeting of basic needs and the social conditions that shape those meanings. It calls for a look at the economic context of childhood in the United States.

Being poor is about being left out of what your society tells people they could expect if they were included. This is relative poverty. At root, it's a social question. Recently, a child asked me, "When you were growing up were you poor or regular?" That's it precisely, are you poor or regular? Being poor means being negatively different; it means not meeting the basic standards set by your society. It is not so much a matter of what you have, but what you don't. Many first-person accounts of life in an earlier era seem to say, "I never knew we were poor until . . ." For example, a priest tells the story of spending a day at school putting together "poor baskets" for Christmas, only to be shocked the next day when one was delivered to his house. "I never knew we were poor until that day," he recounts.

Poverty now has messages that were largely absent in the past, and it is tied up in feelings of shame. Moreover, a poor family faces terrible obstacles to participating in the monetarized economy. In some societies that is only one minor problem. But it becomes an ever-bigger problem as monetarization proceeds and resources in the nonmonetarized economy become inaccessible and devalued, and more and more of the activities of daily life are being sucked into the cash economy. Here's how our two economies work.

Two Economies

Mom feels your head and says you feel warm, so she takes your temperature and sends you to bed early because you're coming down with a cold. Dad tells you to wash your hands before you come to the dinner table. Grandma takes care of you while mom's at work. Dad sits with you in the morning until the school bus comes. Your older brother fixes your bicycle and repaints it. Your sister's backyard garden yields tomatoes for dinner and flowers to bring to the teacher. The man next door shows your dad how to fix the leaky gutter on your house. Your mom shows his wife how to repair a hole in her sweater. The kids down the street put on a puppet show. You organize a ball game in the street on your block. All this represents a great deal of economic activity, and yet all of it is invisible to conventional economic accounting systems. None of it appears in the Gross National Product (GNP); as far as traditional economists are concerned, its value is $0.00.

What will it take for these goods and services to show up in the GNP? Mom drives you to the HMO office, where the nurse uses a disposable plastic cover ($1.50) over the electronic thermometer to take your temperature ($30.00). The home health video sent home from school ($19.95) admonishes you to use disposable moist towels ($1.40 each) to clean your hands before each meal. Dad drops you off at the child care center ($10.00), from which you are later bused to school in the morning, then from school back to the center in the afternoon for a few hours ($20.00), until your mom picks you up after work. Your older brother helps you bring your bicycle into the shop to be fixed and repainted ($37.98). Your sister picks up some tomatoes ($1.75) and flowers ($5.95) at the supermarket on her way home from school. The neighbor refers you to a good roof repair service to fix your leaky gutters ($195.00), and in return, your mom tells his wife about the clothing repair service at the cleaners ($10.00). The kids down the street invite you in to catch the Disney Channel on cable TV ($29.95 per month), and in return, you let them try your new video game cartridge ($32.50). Total contribution to the GNP: $396.18.

What all this comes down to is that the GNP measures the *cash* transactions involving goods and services that take place in a society—the monetarized economy. The GNP does not measure the nonmonetarized economy—activities don't "count" if no money changes hands. But a great deal of work, production, and business is taken care of in the nonmonetarized economy, particularly when it comes to the goods and services that really matter in the development of children. For example, according to some estimates, until recently, more than 90 percent of basic health care and child care took place in the nonmonetarized economy (that is, within families and neighborhoods). These goods and services are no less real for being nonmonetarized, despite the fact that they are largely invisible in conventional models of economic accounting.

As a result, if we simply shift activities from the nonmonetarized economy into the monetarized economy (that is, attach a dollar price tag to them), it looks like economic growth—but in reality, it's only a switch in accounting. What is more, this process can hide real losses and even make them appear as gains. For example, if children can no longer swim free in the local lake and must use a swimming pool because the lake has become polluted, their families must pay money for the pool use, and the GNP shows an increase. However, there may actually be a decrease in enjoyment, because some families may not be able to afford the price of what was once free. That puts pressure on families and accentuates the human costs of being poor. If you lack cash in a monetarized society, you will *feel* poor, because you will not be able to have many of the pleasures (and necessities) of life. In the nonmonetarized economy, transactions involve mutual services—and time, of which everyone starts with an equal supply. If you have access to a strong nonmonetarized economy, you may not feel poor even though you lack cash.

Expectations and the Distribution of Income

The total wealth of families, indeed of the entire society, is the same regardless of how that wealth is distributed between the monetarized and nonmonetarized economy. Conventional economic analysis has trouble dealing with this, however, since only transactions in the monetarized economy count in the GNP. The result is pressure to move things into the monetarized economy. As I described before, this move appears to stimulate economic growth, because the GNP increases and someone can claim credit in the form of cash profit. But it also puts financial pressure on families, particularly lower-middle-class and low-income families.

As a result of monetarization, families find it takes more and more income to meet basic needs—at least what our society defines as basic needs. Whether it's paper diapers instead of cloth, cable television instead of broadcast, driving to work and school instead of walking, or a dishwasher instead of a sink, life today costs more in large measure because more and more of it lies within the cash economy. This is a peculiar form of inflation.

One result is that few families can afford to own a house on one income, and owning a house is one of the foundations of middle-class family life in America. It is valuable for the family and for the community. It is valuable psychologically and socially. It motivates investment in the community and enhances stability, because home owners have a stake in the well-being of the community. Home ownership builds financial equity that can be cashed in or borrowed against to fund important activities such as college education for children. It is part of the bedrock of middle-class economic life, whereas poverty is social quicksand.

Even two-parent families struggle in the cash economy. In 1960, 61 percent of all two-parent families managed on one income. In 1990, only 21 percent did. That is a dramatic change. Few individual earners—particularly women alone with children—can generate enough income to buy what needs buying in our economy and make the investment of time and energy that children demand if they are to grow up robust and pro-social. This shackles single-parent households with a heavy burden, and it particularly affects young families. What is more, in the 1960s, a minimum wage put a family of three above the poverty level. In 1990, it put a family 25 percent below that line. It's little wonder that in 1990, 40 percent of young families were poor. Their plight is compounded by the shifting of resources away from low-income rental housing. In 1970, there were 6.8 million low-income rental units available and 6.4 million low-income families. By 1990, there were 5.5 million low-income units and 9.6 million low-income families.[4] This is bad news for families because it deprives them of a home.

Adults and children are in this together. Canvas sneakers won't do; leather running shoes are required equipment (at triple the price). Child care is a multibillion dollar industry. Private lessons are a staple of the childhood experience for middle-class families. Cable TV and VCRs are basic cultural equipment. Walking to work is a luxury few can afford. Most people invest large amounts of cash commuting to a job where they try to earn enough income to keep the whole complex system going because their sense of self-worth is tied to their place in the consumer economy.

Economic disturbances that occur now are more closely related to social toxicity for many reasons. One is that people must face them in the wake of the economic track record of the post–World War II era. The sustained growth of the decades after the war led most Americans, except perhaps the chronically impoverished underclass, to *expect* material affluence on a mass scale that is unprecedented in human history.

Furthermore, the conventional practice of confining serious

analysis to the monetarized economy, without regard to its relationship with the nonmonetarized economy, can hide troubling problems. For example, GNP grew by 2.2 percent in the 1980s. Good news for families? Not really. The bad news is that child poverty doubled in that period, so that by the end of the 1980s more children lived in poverty than at the start of the decade. More to the point is the finding that income (in constant dollars) for the lower 40 percent of Americans declined during the 1980s (by 4.4 percent for the bottom 20 percent of the population).[5]

What's more, young families suffered the most severe declines in income. These declines were most evident for families in which the breadwinners had a track record of educational failure. In particular, families headed by high school dropouts experienced a 17.3 percent decline in income during the 1980s.

At the same time, income for educationally successful families (that is, those with college-educated breadwinners) increased significantly. For families in the top 20 percent of the income structure, income increased by 28.9 percent (and for the top 1 percent it increased by 74 percent!).[6] Compounding this uneven distribution have been tax policies that relieve upper-income taxpayers while increasing the burden of lower-income taxpayers.

At one time (not that long ago in our national history), it made sense to use the unemployment rate as a good indicator of family well-being, because it was taken for granted that being employed meant having enough income to meet basic needs for children. But a report prepared for Congress concluded that half the new jobs created during the 1980s paid a wage that was less than the poverty figure for a family of four, even if held full-time for twelve months out of the year.[7] This trend continues in the 1990s (as does the trend noted earlier in which the minimum wage fails to raise a family above the poverty line). The point is that lowered unemployment rates may mislead us into thinking that things are improving for families. But if holding a full-time job still means poverty for that worker's children, then the numbers are giving us a false picture of what is really going on. This problem is particularly serious for single-parent, female-headed households, because of women's lower average earnings.

Some economists argue that the basis used for calculating the poverty level itself is flawed because of the disproportionate rise in the costs of food, housing, and child care, which consume a greater proportion of income at the lower than the higher end of the scale.[8] Others contend that this increase in costs is offset by the fact that noncash medical benefits available to the poor are not included in the standard calculations of the poverty level. But however we calculate the official definition, poverty remains a serious psychological and moral problem for U.S. families. Poverty is a problem for the entire society as well, because of the adverse consequences to children and the disruption they bring to the social fabric as a result.

Right now, we are passing the buck for these problems until it stops on the doorstep of those who are charged with the responsibility of child protective services, remedial education, and other human services. All these agencies were designed originally to be a *last* resort rather than the principal resource base for developing children, but they're coping as best they can. However, we cannot expect child welfare services to compensate for our society's deteriorating foundations indefinitely, or to clean up the mess of social toxicity.

In contrast to most of the societies of Western Europe, we have not put into place the basic elements of a modern social welfare state—universal access to health care, a livable minimum wage, direct child subsidies.[9] Thus, poverty is the vehicle through which the deficiencies in our economic thinking and action are manifest.

I recall sitting next to a foreign visitor one afternoon on a flight to Seattle. At the time, the newspapers were covering the national debate over President Clinton's health care plan. My seatmate was reading the newspaper and appeared to be having some difficulty understanding what he was reading. Finally, he leaned over and asked for my help. "Perhaps I am not understanding," he said, somewhat apologetically, "but this article seems to be saying that thirty million people in your country have no health insurance.

Surely, that cannot be true," he continued. I nodded my head forlornly and replied, "Yes. That's what it says." "Don't you care for your people?" he asked, somewhat shocked at our national callousness. This may explain why correlations between measures of income or socioeconomic status and basic child outcomes are often higher in the United States than in other modern societies.[10] It is one thing for social class differences to predict matters of style and taste—for example, whether you watch opera or *Roseanne*, drink fine vintage wine or wine coolers, or wear blue blazers or overalls. It is quite another when social class—and poverty in particular—predicts who lives and who dies, and who is robust and who is disabled. Low income is a better predictor of child development problems in the United States than in other countries because our social policies tend to exaggerate rather than minimize the impact of family income on access to human services such as health care and child care. As the foreign visitor said, "Don't we care about our people?"

Of course, even a financially affluent social environment may lack the kind of enduring support systems that children and adolescents need to provide positive role models, caring adult supervision, and a sense of personal validation. The same may be true for the parents, who may feel acutely embarrassed to admit difficulty with their children in a community in which there is a presumption of competence and high expectations for achievement. However, the social toxicity that comes from unsupportive communities is seen most clearly among the poor, and particularly among the concentrations of poverty that have come to dominate many inner-city areas. Here risk factors accumulate. Opportunity diminishes. Crime and despair flourish.

What It Would Take to Give Poor Children a Chance

If there is a lesson of the 1980s, it is that in the current economic structure and without substantial intervention, the rich really do get richer while the poor really do get poorer. With a return to power of the ideology of the 1980s in the elections of November 1994, the process may well accelerate in the latter half of the 1990s. The internal situation in the United States thus mirrors the global choices we make between more luxuries for the "haves" versus more necessities for the "have nots."

Average income is not the issue. Average income rose 14.5 percent during the 1980s. If we adjust the Bureau of Labor Statistics numbers to account for inflation since the data were last compiled in the mid 1980s, a family of four living at a "high" level requires about $48,000; the same family living at a "lower" (struggling) level requires about $25,000, and the same family living at the "poverty" level requires about $14,000. How do these numbers match up with the realities of family income? By 1989, half of America's families had an income of $33,974. That's good. But at the same time the average income of the lowest 20 percent was $7,725—much too little—while the average income of the highest 20 percent was $105,209—well above the comfort level.

It may well be impossible to increase earnings for all three groups—affluent, struggling, and poor—at the same time. If so, what should be our highest priority? Is subsidizing families below the $14,000 level sufficient? Once that is achieved (or before), should the goal of policy be to bring as much of the population as possible up to $25,000? Or should it be to enhance the prospects of those who have reached the $48,000 level?

The goal of increasing income for those at the bottom is much more germane to improving the well-being of children and the prevention of developmental risks. Each dollar below the struggling level has a negative effect on the well-being of children. It increases the odds that a child will suffer from some form of physical, psychological, or social problem. Each dollar above the adequate figure ($25,000 for the 1990s) has only a marginal payoff in terms of child welfare and development. Each dollar added to the affluent income ($48,000 in the 1990s) may have no value whatsoever for overall child welfare. Expressed statistically, reducing poverty is associated with improved outcomes for children, while increasing affluence is not.[11]

Conventional economic models of growth do not recognize the critical quality of this distinction. If the GNP grows by $1 billion, conventional economic models do not see any intrinsic reason to be concerned with whether those added dollars raise incomes at the bottom or increase wealth at the top. Unfortunately, conventional thinking about economic growth seems to parallel the thinking of a character in a *New Yorker* cartoon from the 1980s: "The poor are getting poorer, but with the rich getting richer it all averages out in the end."

Economic issues play a very large role in the dynamics of social toxicity. To the degree to which the community's day-to-day life is monetarized, families will be drawn or driven into the cash economy. If local government and philanthropic institutions remain aloof from this process, those who cannot generate sufficient cash income to participate in basic activities will become ever poorer. This is what happened in Brazil's boom of the 1970s to 1980s: 80 percent of the population became poorer. While GNP increased substantially, overall quality of life suffered, infant mortality rose, and millions of children were abandoned by their families.

What should we expect? Along one path lies an increasing return to the Dickensian model: extreme disparities of both income and justice, with the lower end of the spectrum mired in desperate poverty. Central and South America offer many case studies of what this would mean. Brazil is a prime example. Along another path lies a commitment to meet the basic needs of all of the people all of the time, regardless of race, creed, national origin, or income-generating capacity. Put another way, the goal is preventing poverty and strengthening middle-class society as the foundation for a more socially benign environment for children. We may debate whether paper and plastic diapers (which are pernicious for the environment) are needs for *anyone*, but we must define as needs those resources that clearly contribute to family stability, security, and time together, and to basic academic achievement and socialization in the family and the school. In sum, we must work to achieve economic fairness in matters of housing and health.

What Can We Do?

To change the socially toxic situation, we can commit ourselves as citizens to public policies designed to meet two challenges—one intellectual, the other spiritual. The intellectual challenge is to insist upon analytic models that address both the monetarized and the nonmonetarized economies. This challenge strains our resources, because so much of our existing thinking is rooted in a narrowly monetarized idea of economic life. The cash-based GNP is the dominant model in academia, in government, and in the mass media. However, we must insist that economic analyses in the political arena focus on the total picture, as opposed to gross measures that can hide important inequities. If more and more jobs do not pay enough to meet minimum income standards and do not come with adequate benefits (as is more and more the case), then simply totaling up unemployment and employment data is insufficient. When what looks like economic growth really just measures activities moving from the nonmonetarized to the monetarized economy, then the data can be misleading at best. We cannot think about the problem of providing adequate income and employment when we cannot even decide what they are or how to measure them.

The spiritual challenge is to put our money where our values ought to be, to make reducing poverty and reinforcing middle-class society our number one national priority. This means more than just handing out welfare checks, of course. It means building successful families, competent schools, and positive communities in which good jobs exist to meet the basic human need to work and people are prepared to perform those jobs competently. It means, again, an accounting system that takes seriously the total wealth of families (in both the monetarized and nonmonetarized economies) and their basic need for affirmation, respect, and regard. Shielding children from the effects of poverty means ensuring that high-quality health care and schooling are available to *all* families, particularly families with young children, regardless of family income. If we make a commitment to this access as a matter of human rights, all we have left to face are the logistical issues. This is the true nature of government's contract with America.

Beyond these public policy issues involved in the transition to a sustainable society are the personal issues of family finance and home economics. There is much we can do to improve the economic picture of families with low incomes if we remember to consider the nonmonetarized economy. Growing and preparing food at home is one way to improve economic resources without affecting cash income. There are a whole host of such measures, measures that include smart technology to make homes energy and heat efficient, measures that can reduce the impact of low income per se on the home economics of a family. If such activities are part of a broader community mobilization, they can offset many of the social effects of poverty as well and move us toward a sustainable society.[12]

Chapter Nine

Thriving

Taking Responsibility for the Future

We want our children to do more than just survive, more than just struggle through. We want them to thrive. Even though the social environment is toxic, we can do much within the home to help our children thrive, and we can help all children thrive by working for change at the community and national levels—changing schools, preventing poverty, and counterbalancing the barrage of nastiness and violence that poisons the way our children think and feel every day. In addition, we can learn how to focus our efforts by understanding just how risk factors weigh on our children.

Weighing the Risk

Life is never risk free. Most children must contend with risk factors of one sort or another, some as a result of the ongoing conditions of life, others as a consequence of catastrophic events. Some children face chronic poverty, for example, while others must cope with the unexpected death of a parent or sibling. Some must contend with living in a crime-infested neighborhood; others experience a once-in-a-lifetime disaster. And some children must cope with all of these at once.

When I look back on the children I knew growing up, I can catalog the risk factors we faced in my neighborhood. Several of us had fathers who were unemployed at one time or another as the economy went up and down during the 1950s and 1960s. Some of us had physical problems of one sort or another—as I think back and do a house-by-house review of the neighbors up and down our street, I can remember quite a few: a cleft lip, malformed legs requiring phys-ical therapy, minor retardation, asthma. I can also remember bad things that happened to some of us. One boy was hit by a car while riding on his bicycle; another developed a stutter. A girl up the street got pregnant, a boy across the street suffered from dwarfism. My best friend got rheumatic fever and had to be very careful about overtiring himself forever afterward. Two families didn't have fathers—we never found out why. Another family fought a lot—the girl of that family seemed sad or mad much of the time. Looking back on it, I suspect there were several rocky marriages on our block.

But we had a lot going for us, too. No one ever starved. We always had a roof over our heads. We lived in a stable community, and it was safe to be out on the streets, day or night. The schools were staffed by people who knew what they were doing and were committed to teaching. Neighbors generally kept an eye on things—if only to gossip about each other. They even formed a block organization on Merton Avenue, where we all lived—"The Merton Mob," as it was called. By and large, parents loved their kids—often fiercely enough to complain to the parents of any child who did them an injustice. Though many of us had ethnic sur-names, Italian and Irish mainly, we were definitely not part of a minority group experiencing blatant discrimination. We had risk factors, but we had resources and opportunities too. We faced chal-lenges, but we coped. To the best of my knowledge, none of the kids I grew up with succumbed to criminal or self-destructive behavior. There was no significant drug culture to fall prey to. No one had a gun, so none of our arguments ever terminated in a fatality. Our school was small, so even most of the academically marginal stu-dents finished high school. We coped.

What differentiates children and youth today from the kids of my childhood? It's not that we were resilient and they aren't. It's not that kids today face risk factors and our lives were risk free. So what is it, then? I think the difference lies in the fact that children and youth today often face an overwhelming *accumulation* of risks in their families and communities, and do so with greatly reduced access to compensating opportunities due to the psychologically toxic nature of the social environment they inhabit. This idea of risk accumulation bears further attention because it provides the necessary context for thinking about how we can promote resilience in today's children and youth, how we can enhance resources and opportunities to counterbalance risk.

Risk Accumulates; Opportunity Ameliorates

Risk accumulates; opportunity ameliorates. These two propositions are more than just a fear and a hope. Each is grounded in an emerging body of child development research. It turns out that the presence or absence of any single risk factor rarely tells us much about a child's prospects in life.

Rather, it is the accumulation of risk factors that jeopardizes development. The presence of one or two risk factors does not developmentally disable children, but the accumulation of three, four, or more can overwhelm a child—particularly when these risk factors accumulate without a parallel accumulation of opportunity factors.[1] Once overwhelmed, children are likely to be highly sensitive to the socially toxic influences surrounding them.

Give me one tennis ball and I can toss it up and down with ease. Give me two and I can still manage easily. Add a third and it takes special skill to juggle them. Make it four and I will drop them all. So it is with risk factors. Yet this can be good news for us as parents. If there are one or two risk factors beyond our immediate control, they need not be destructive. At the same time, they should be an urgent warning, telling us to protect the child from any further risks.

As risk factors accumulate, intellectual development suffers and children cannot bring to bear cognitive strength in mastering the challenges they face. In a study of four-year-olds conducted by psychologist Arnold Sameroff, children with fewer than three risk factors had above-average IQ scores of 112; children with four had below-average IQ scores of 93.[2]

A child whose risk accumulates starts to achieve less. As a result of lowered achievement, that child learns to devalue himself or herself. As a result of such devaluation, that child comes to lack the reservoir of self-esteem needed to keep positive momentum going when the going gets tough. Impaired parent-child relations lead children to feel alienated and angry, and to reorient to peers, oftentimes peers who share their feelings of abandonment or rage, and who might influence them away from socially responsible values and behavior.

Developmental harm arises when risk factors accumulate and overwhelm coping capacity. Psychiatrist Michael Rutter concludes that this risk increases fourfold and then tenfold as additional risk factors accumulate beyond two or three.[3]

It is worth taking some time to look at the Sameroff study, which provides one of the clearest demonstrations.[4] He and his colleagues explored the relationship between a child's IQ and the presence of eight risk factors (including poverty, father absence, low parental education, a rigid and punitive childrearing style, minority group status, parental substance abuse, maternal mental illness, and large family size). Figure 9.1 presents the results.

These results make it clear there is little effect on the child's intellectual competence with up to two risk factors—*any* two. In a way that's quite remarkable. Little kids are not suffering *intellectual* effects by age four of living in poverty with a drug-abusing mother, or experiencing father absence and being in a minority group, or of being reared by crazy, punitive parents (setting aside for a moment any *emotional* effects of these factors). The big effect is noted at three or four risk factors, with only a modest further decline after five. That's when IQ is low—low enough to be a problem. We can use these results as a general strategy for approaching the topic of developmental risk as it affects children. We can do so with the recognition that we need not make life risk free for children to pro-

Figure 9.1. IQ as a Function of Risk Accumulation Among Four-Year-Old Children.

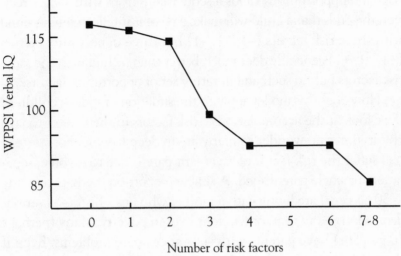

Number of risk factors

Note: WPPSI Verbal IQ is an individually administered test of the child's intelligence.

Source: Sameroff, Seifer, Barocas, Zax, and Greenspan, 1987.

tect them from serious harm, but rather must prevent the accumulation of risk beyond the coping capacity of the child.

But there's more to it than just the accumulation of risk; there's the compensating force of opportunity. It doesn't make sense to categorize the experience of children in terms of "risk" and "not risk." Some children experience more than "not risk," they experience *opportunity*. It's more than that their father is not absent, their father is intensely involved with them. It's more than that their mother is avoiding alcoholism, their mother is a model of how to manage alcohol effectively (and by implication, everything else as well). It's more than being not poor, they have the resources to open doors. In short, it's more than the absence of risk, it's the presence of opportunities. Put simply, while some children score "–1" (risk factor) and others score "0" (absence of risk), a third group scores "+1" (an opportunity factor).

Psychologist Carl Dunst has translated this approach into research extending Sameroff's study. He reports that adding up the risks and opportunities yields a score that tells us with some precision the odds that a child will make a go of it intellectually. A child with three risk factors (−1, −1, −1) but three opportunity factors (+1, +1, +1) generally does much better than a child with the same risk factors but no such ameliorating set of opportunity factors.[5]

How does this model apply to the situation of today's children? If we look at the accumulation of risk factors in the lives of today's children, it's no wonder so many are in deep trouble. For starters, half suffer the risk factor of an absent parent due to divorce, separation, or single parenthood. A sizable proportion (perhaps as many as 30 percent) are living with a mother who has a history of serious depression. More than one in four lives in poverty. Many (perhaps 10 percent) have parents with substance abuse problems. Even if these risk factors were spread evenly and randomly across the population, many children would end up in the danger zone of risk accumulation. And the risks are not spread evenly. For example, more than 50 percent of African-American children are poor in single-parent households. A recent study reported that 28 percent of parents on welfare (and who are thus poor and single parents) have substance abuse problems. The children who live with these accumulations of risk have heightened vulnerability to the toxins in the social environment beyond their families.[6]

Of all children, children burdened by an accumulation of risk factors most need a safe, stable neighborhood; but neighborhood safety and stability have declined most in the areas they live. They most need the special opportunities that a small school offers; but they are in large schools. They have the least capacity to resist the drug culture; but they are surrounded by drugs and the life of the drug economy. They have the most need for easy access to the economy through unskilled labor that can generate income enough to meet basic needs, but they have a hard time finding jobs at all—and the jobs they do find generally leave them in poverty.

Consider two brief illustrations of just how powerful and important social conditions are in shaping individual development. First, genetically identical twins separated at birth and growing up in *similar* communities end up with similar IQs (correlated .88), while genetically identical twins separated but living in *dissimilar* communities end up with IQs much less alike (correlated .26).[7] Second, children who are developmentally delayed (low Developmental Quotient—DQ) at four months of age and receive no significant remedial intervention are four times as likely to be intellectually delayed (low IQ) at four years of age than are similarly delayed children who receive such intervention.[8] Does X cause Y? It depends. It depends upon social context. People can overcome a great deal if the social environment favors them in this struggle.

We have a mission. That mission is to do all we can to reduce risk and increase opportunity in the lives of our children. One place to start is with identity, the very definition of a person.

Affirmation and Identity

As I've said, children thrive on acceptance. Rejection corrodes and damages the sense of self-worth in much the way that cancer damages the body; it twists a child's outlook and makes every action painful. Thus rejected children and youth are in jeopardy. They are prone to antisocial and self-destructive behavior as well as negative self-concepts. Accepted children, on the other hand, learn to see themselves as strong and surrounded by others whom they can trust—a social map that leads to a much better adulthood than can be found following the map generated by rejection.

Thriving Is More Than Just Coping

The good news about human development is that people can adapt to anything. The bad news about human development is that people can adapt to anything. I think it's very important to recognize this truth about human experience. Human adaptability allows us as a species to survive under an extremely wide range of conditions—desert and tundra, forest and swamp, war and peace, rich and poor, sickness and health.

But that same adaptability means that we will tolerate the existence of horrible conditions, and justify our tolerance on the grounds that people survive those conditions—and even continue to reproduce. But coping can be costly. Survival is not the only measure of success. We must go further to examine issues of human quality. Human beings are more than just bodies. Life is more than just breathing and eating. Beyond coping is thriving.

I think of this often when I visit war zones and other places of horror around the world. Children coped with the Nazi concentration camps during the 1930s and 1940s. Children coped with the Khmer Rouge death camps in Cambodia during the 1970s. Children coped with the systematic brutality of the Renamo guerrillas in Mozambique in the 1980s. Children coped with the ethnic cleansing in the former Yugoslavia in the 1990s. Children coped with the Vietnamese detention camps in Hong Kong. Children cope with life in inner city war zones. What are the costs of this sort of coping? People coped, but at what cost?

Robert Coles noted this in his study of the political life of children: under conditions of violent political crisis *some* children develop a precocious and precious moral sensibility, while others succumb to the moral threat, becoming consumed with desire for revenge and return victimization.[9] This is a central theme as we seek to understand the mediators between danger and trauma, on the one hand, and between danger and moral development, on the other.

This effort must be developmental, in the sense that it concerns itself with the long-term implications of childhood events, not just their immediate consequences. We must see them in light of the child's ongoing efforts to adapt to them, to cope with them. Thus, for example, recent longitudinal analyses of the impact of divorce on children suggest a "sleeper effect," with life adjustment problems emerging ten or more years after marital dissolution.[10]

Coping with a highly stressful environment can lead to long-term mental health problems, and problems in an individual's philosophy of life, even when the child has access to parental protection in the short term. This is evident in economically stressful situations, even if they do not include acute danger. For example, studies of the impact of having been a child during the Great Depression of the 1930s in the United States reveal effects seen decades later in the life course of adults, particularly for males.[11]

Children forced to cope with chronic stress may do so in ways that end up causing problems later. In extreme cases (such as living in a concentration camp, an inner city war zone, or an abusive family) the psychopathological dimensions of such adaptation are now widely recognized—most notably PTSD and even multiple personality disorder. The social dimensions are equally worthy of attention, however. Children (and parents) may cope with chronic stress by adopting a strategy of withdrawal.

This withdrawal may involve deliberate physical isolation, withdrawing from the community because of concern about its theoretical (or real) dangers. It can take an extreme form, as when parents refuse to let children play outdoors for fear of kidnapping, or it can be a simple matter of preferring the television to direct participation in the world. It can also be an emotional withdrawal, a refusal to contemplate or care about anyone else's needs. In either case, people who cope by withdrawing become less effective as human beings, and the social environments where they live become more toxic for everyone, including themselves. The vicious cycle continues.

Similarly, in their efforts to cope with the fear they feel for their children's well-being, parents may adopt a very restrictive and punitive style of discipline in an effort to keep the child from falling under the influence of negative forces in the social environment, such as gangs. Unfortunately, this approach to dealing with social toxicity is likely to have the result of heightening aggression on the child's part, with one consequence being a difficulty in succeeding in nonviolent settings. Ironically, these parents may be driving children into the arms of the very gangs they fear.

Another consequence of such a coercive approach may be to endorse and accept violence as the modus operandi for social control, which in turn rationalizes the gangs' use of violence as their dominant tactic for social influence. Holding the child back from negative forces through punitive restrictiveness is generally a much less successful strategy than promoting positive alternatives to the subculture feared by the parent.[12]

In all three of these examples—withdrawal, coercive discipline, deliberate in-home violence—the adaptation is well intentioned and may appear to be practical and sensible, but its side effects may be detrimental in the long run. The onus here, of course, is on the social forces that create and sustain stressful conditions in the family's environment. These forces increase the stressfulness of being a parent, and make decision making much harder. It does little good to blame people for flawed adaptation to the stress of today's toxic social environment. Instead, let us look at what children do to cope successfully with challenge and risk, and consider what parents (and others in the community) can do to support them and create conditions in which they can thrive.

Successful Coping and Resilience: Seven Themes

When we look at all the research that has been done in an effort to understand why some children overcome difficult life circumstances while others do not, seven important themes emerge:[13]

• *Personal anchors.* Children need stable positive emotional relationships with at least one parent or other reference person. This is the single most important resource you can have to promote resilience in childhood: having someone who is crazy about you. Mom. Dad. Gramps. Nana. Whoever. Early attachment relationships are the first lessons in what the world is all about. When they teach trust children are off to a good start in life.

I understood this (or thought I did) when I was a graduate student in child development many years ago because I studied the research and because I was attached to my own parents. But when I became a parent myself I learned much more about it. The bond I feel with my children has been an invaluable teacher. To see the smile that comes from a baby for you because you are *you*, and to see what that recognition permits the child to do, is very instructive (to say the least).

Early positive relationships teach you to trust and respond and feel and pay attention. On the other hand, if your early relationships are unreliable or negative, they teach you to fear and turn away and become numb and turn inward. Like all human developments, the development of the capacity to form and sustain stable, positive attachments is not irremediably harmed if early experiences with relationships are negative. But if your early experience is poor it gets harder and harder, and takes a more and more skilled and loving adult to compensate. In fact, it may require the efforts of a trained psychotherapist to achieve that recovery.

• *Cognitive competence.* At least an average level of intelligence provides an important resource in coping successfully. It makes sense that children who are capable of analyzing their social environment effectively will stand a better chance of mastering it. Such children will have better access to the resources of the culture through school, and will be more likely to avoid self-defeating strategies for coping.

Smarter kids are more resilient. Thus, anything that suppresses the intellectual development of children, particularly in situations of high risk, compounds the threat posed by those risks. This provides an important link between intervention programs aimed at improving intellectual development and larger efforts to help children cope.

• *Success.* Children who have a track record of success are more likely to internalize the belief that they are capable of succeeding each time they meet a challenge. This reservoir of self-confidence is a vital resource for anyone, but especially for children who must demonstrate their ability to overcome adversity again and again and again. Part and parcel of this is learning a wide range of coping skills. Thus, boys who incorporate traditionally feminine traits and girls who incorporate traditionally masculine traits are more successful than more one-dimensional children.

But we should remember that this is not just a matter of just being told you're wonderful, of "feeling good about yourself." It's more a matter of *concluding* that you are competent and valuable by having experiences of validation and mastery. It takes genuine instances of self-efficacy to lead to a corresponding self-confidence and positive self-esteem.

• *Active coping.* In general, it seems that children who actively seek to master challenges as they come along seem to do better than children who passively react to stress. This suggests that we should do all we can with children—particularly children who are temperamentally inclined to be passive—to encourage active strategies.

Children need emotional support, but part of that support is to help them face up to life's challenges. One way to do this, I believe, is to encourage children to view themselves as leaders. I often find myself telling children—including my own—that it is insufficient to simply "not go along." That's important, but it is more important to actively lead in the right direction. Helping children incorporate this concept of leadership into their social maps of self is vitally important to overcome the stress of living in a socially toxic environment.

• *Positive temperament.* Life is not particularly fair, and temperamental characteristics—largely inborn traits—do play a role in coping and resilience. Some children come into the world more active and more sociable than others, and some are more inclined to passive withdrawal. Resilient children tend to seek out potentially useful adults and draw them in, and thus win more help and support than their passive cousins.

I know this from visits to refugee camps around the world. Some children appeal. They are the ones I would take home with me if I could. Others hang back or in some other way put me off. Even if we accept that these differences have their origins in inborn temperament, there may be ways to increase this sociability and activity by teaching social skills to children. We've made progress in helping shy children become more outgoing; we need to develop similar techniques for helping passive children become better able to take control of their lives.

• *Social climate.* Children do best in an open, supportive educational climate, and with parental models of behavior that encourage constructive coping with problems. Resilience arises from a combination of the child and the environment. It's not just a matter of some children being invulnerable and others being vulnerable. One important influence is the home, to be sure. It helps a lot if the home gives messages of affirmation and support, messages that show and tell children that they can handle what life throws at them.

Another influence lies in the institutions outside the home, most notably in the school. Some schools do a better job of building and sustaining resilience than others. Successful schools provide models of coping. In Michael Rutter's view, they encourage a *planful* approach to life; that is, they teach children that they can think through situations and take steps to improve the future, academically and socially.[14]

These schools offer children a chance to process and reflect upon their experiences, to work through the important issues in their lives. Like effective parents, they send a clear message of caring, and include respect for the child's thoughts and words in their definition of caring.

• *Additional support.* Schools and parents are not the only participants in the child's life. Other adults acting as individuals can play an important role in fostering resilience. These people are the child's neighborhood and community. They play their role by offering something extra—perhaps taking the child under their wing when a child's family is in disarray or preoccupied with some crisis, offering the child a special opportunity to develop a talent or interest that can become a sustaining force for the child, or intervening on the child's behalf with parents or school officials. All this presupposes that the child has access to the community beyond the family, of course, and that children are not so afraid of predators that they don't take advantage of the social support out there.

This is what resilience and coping are all about—meeting challenges and mastering them. If children can muster their internal and external resources, if we give them half a chance, they will respond. Human beings are motivated and capable of restoring themselves to equilibrium when thrown off balance. In more formal terms, children are "self-righting systems."

The keys to this capacity are intelligence, self-worth, activity, attachment, social support, and education. The challenges of living in a socially toxic environment demand much of children, but children can handle them if they are resilient. Little kids can stand tall, and in doing so they can grow wise and achieve heightened moral development. Moral growth and social development are possible, even in the face of a socially toxic environment.

I believe we are waking up to the problems for children posed by our socially toxic environment. I recently spoke to a group of midwestern professionals, civic leaders, and parents about the themes expressed and explored in this book. At the end of my allotted forty-five minutes, I asked them to let me know by a show of hands if what I was saying made sense to them and if it seemed to describe what they observed in their community. Without hesitation, every hand in the room shot up, and heads began to nod. I had touched a responsive chord in them.

But it wasn't always so. More than two decades earlier, as a young graduate student, I listened while my mentor, Urie Bronfenbrenner, laid out his analysis of where things were headed in North America. Working from his then newly published book, *Two Worlds of Childhood*, he discussed the growing threats to the social and moral development of children.[15] He sought to raise the alarm much as Rachel Carson had done for the physical environment in her *Silent Spring* a generation before.[16] But his alarm fell on deaf ears with the midwestern audience. "Maybe that stuff is a problem in New York and Los Angeles," many of them said, "but not here in our community!" Now, I was following up on Bronfenbrenner's prophetic message with an accounting of the way bad things had gotten worse, and the audience was fully in accord with the analysis.

Talking with Bronfenbrenner about this a few days later, his response was sobering. There was no selfish "I told you so" pleasure, only a sadness about how far things had come, perhaps how far things had to come before people were ready to see and listen. "Yes," he said. "Back then the problem would have been much more manageable because there were still so many resources in place to do something about it. Now?" his voice trailed off, but the look of worry on his face spoke volumes.

We are in deep trouble. Our children are in deep trouble. But despair is not going to solve the problems. A colleague of mine used to say that to manage in the twentieth century it was necessary to function as a kind of ambulatory schizophrenic. By that he meant that each of us must recognize the craziness of our situation, the apparently insurmountable problems we face, and yet go about the business of doing better, of leading a good life, of taking responsibility for the future. Bruno Bettelheim put it this way: "We all survive on trust and hope, not on fact."[17]

I think that is true here and now. Each child born is a new opportunity. Each family can make choices and decisions that strengthen children and strike a small blow against the social toxicity that surrounds us. Citizens can put their money and their voices behind programs and policies aimed at detoxifying the social environment: establishing smaller schools; drawing closer ties between children and the community; defusing violence; resisting nastiness; turning off the television; being strong for children; making adult relationships work as well as possible in the child's best interest.

Parents and professionals can work together to strengthen children *and* to detoxify the social environment in which those children will experience adolescence.

In the twenty-first century, the next generation will look back at the closing years of the twentieth century and take stock of the way we responded, now that we know what is going on, now that we have the concepts we need to put together the pieces of evidence about the toxicity of the social environment for children. There will be a full accounting. They will ask what we did in response to what we knew. What will be our answer?

What Can We Do?

Children begin their acquaintance with the written world through alphabet books, the ABCs of literacy. In the Resources section, I present an ABC for grownups—a list of specific things that we can do to create a world where our children can thrive . . . and so can we.

Resources

What We Can Do from A to Z

AFFIRMATION AND ACCEPTANCE are the building blocks for a child's positive identity. Here are some resources that will help you learn how to offer this affirmation effectively:

Lillian Katz has written an excellent booklet on building self-esteem on a firm foundation, and you can purchase a copy by writing to ERIC/EECE, University of Illinois, 805 West Pennsylvania Avenue, Urbana, IL 61801–4897. Their phone number is (800) 583–4135. Ask for "Distinctions Between Self-Esteem and Narcissism: Implications for Practice."

The Just For Kids! program at the Cornell University Family Life Development Center is committed to preventing and dealing with rejection and other forms of psychological maltreatment. You can write to them at Just For Kids, FLDC, G-20 MVR, Cornell University, Ithaca, NY 14853–4401.

The Institute for Mental Health Initiatives focuses on self-esteem, anger management, and other mental health issues. Their address is IMHI, 4545 42nd Street N.W., Suite 311, Washington, DC 20016.

BOYS AND GIRLS each have special vulnerabilities to social toxicity. Boys are most vulnerable to the immediate negative effects of living in a toxic social environment—developmental disabilities, aggression, and other social skills problems. Girls are at special risk for low self-esteem and a crisis in confidence.

We need to increase children's coping skills and protect them from buying into the aggressive and nasty themes in our culture.

This kind of development starts early. Vivian Paley's books reveal much about how to tame little boys. See her *Boys and Girls: Superheroes in the Doll Corner* and *You Can't Say You Can't Play*. Also, see Nancy Carlsson-Paige and Diane Levin's *Who's Calling the Shots* for a practical guide to toys and television for boys *and* girls. We need an ethic that can detoxify institutions and relationships.

All children, but especially boys, need to learn respect for others and tolerance, not through brute parental force, but through a policy of firm but gentle caring. Carol Gilligan's book *In a Different Voice* explores the basis for developing an ethic of caring, and why it takes more time and effort with boys. It also offers guidance in understanding the special needs of girls in a society like ours where the legacy of sexism undermines their development.

CHILDREN COME FIRST! The guiding principle for social policy and family decision making must be that children are the first priority. Investing in our children is the best way to improve the quality of life for the future. Caring for the vulnerable makes good sense. The most vulnerable among us are most affected by social toxicity. Preserving the best in our society hinges upon our making a commitment and investment to care for each and every child—from prenatal care to schooling, from home health visiting programs for everyone to high-quality foster care and adoption programs for those children who require out-of-home placement.

DIVORCE IS TRAUMATIC for children. It has significant effects that often include prolonged emotional pain and sadness, and many of these effects are linked to the poverty that confronts so many children as a result of divorce. If divorce is the best option for the adults involved, then minimize the accumulation of risk factors for the child. Mobilize every possible community and family resource to shield the child from spousal conflict, economic deprivation, dislocation from home, and disruption of other family relationships. Ask the guidance counselor at your child's school about support groups for children going through parental separation and divorce.

ECONOMIC WELL-BEING is best measured by a family's total wealth. Take stock of both the monetarized and the nonmonetarized economy in planning and making decisions for your family and for your community. Consider opportunity costs and figure in the costs to children of putting their needs second to the demands and rewards of the monetarized economy.

FACE-TO-FACE INTERACTION builds relationships. Each of us makes decisions that increase or decrease our regular contact with members of the community in which we live. For example, every use of an automated bank cash machine replaces a face-to-face contact with a human teller. Making use of the human teller is a small pro-social step. Bringing children along when you have face-to-face contact with people in the community boosts the impact of your relationships. Communities do not exist in the abstract. They are made real by day-to-day human interaction, and they waste away when impersonal arrangements replace human contact.

GARDENING teaches important lessons about care, patience, responsibility, hope, and pride. When done as a family or community activity, it contributes to social detoxification. Even in urban settings, it can send important messages to children and build connections across the generations.

HOME HEALTH VISITING shows that the community cares. Home health visiting ought to begin prenatally and continue for the first few years of life for all families everywhere. Join with the Healthy Families America Initiative to meet this goal—you can write them at the National Committee to Prevent Child Abuse, 332 South Michigan Avenue, Suite 1600, Chicago, IL 60604.

INTEGRATION is important along social class as well as racial and ethnic lines. Seek out and embrace diversity as a way to enrich experience and detoxify the social environment. Don't fear it as a threat to your individual identity. Support zoning policies that resist homogenization. Encourage magnet schools that draw diverse children and families together.

JOIN TOGETHER with other parents and adults concerned with the well-being of children. Few parents can succeed as individuals in setting and maintaining high standards for children in the areas of TV watching, supervision, language, and manners. But parents who join together can create social contracts and have adult peer pressure behind them to increase compliance. They can refrain from capitulating to a child's pleas that "everyone else is doing it!"

The National Parent-Teachers Association offers support for parents in setting standards. Write to them at National PTA, 330 North Wabash, Suite 2100, Chicago, IL 60611.

KISS AND MAKE UP. Today's world is full of rough edges and sharp corners. A spirit of reconciliation is essential on every level. Remember the old saying, "If you start out on a journey of revenge, begin by digging two graves—one for your enemy and one for yourself." Conflict-resolution skills are essential to our efforts to detoxify the social environment. Whether the conflict be within families, on the streets, at school, or in the workplace, resolving disputes with respect and affection is a positive step.

For advice on how to proceed, consult the Resolving Conflict Creatively Program, Educators for Social Responsibility, 23 Garden Street, Cambridge, MA 02138.

You can also get help from:

The National Institute for Dispute Resolution, 1726 M Street N.W., Suite 500, Washington, DC 20036; Phone (202) 466–4764

The National Association for Community Mediation, 1726
  M Street N.W., Suite 500, Washington, DC 20036; Phone
  (202) 467–6226

The National Association for Mediation in Education, 1726
  M Street N.W., Suite 500, Washington, DC 20036; Phone
  (202) 466–2772

LIVE LIGHTLY upon the Earth. The environmental movement—
recycling, conservation, species preservation—provides an ideal
starting point for the political education of children. It connects
them with the web of existence, teaches important lessons about
interdependence, and offers concrete things they can do to help.
For an in-depth discussion of how environmental and family issues
mesh, see my book *Toward a Sustainable Society*.

MEN MUST CHANGE. Men must act more responsibly as fathers by
sticking with their kids emotionally and financially, no matter what
happens in their relationship with their child's mother. Men must
also adjust to the many changes in social roles that have come with
growing egalitarianism. If women change and men don't, children
will suffer.

NASTINESS IS AN ENEMY of childhood. The price of freedom from
nastiness is eternal vigilance. Monitor the language, dress, and
behavior of children to protect them from the corrupting influences
of vivid violence on television and the movies, casual profanity, bullying, and cynicism. Set clear and firm limits for household conversation—including your own language. Have a "snap can" into
which *any* family member who violates family rules regarding civility must pay a small fine, with the proceeds going to the family's
favorite charity.

ORGANIZED ACTIVITIES should take second place to free play for
young children. Children explore through play. Free play stimulates

and enhances development. David Elkind's *The Hurried Child* is still a useful resource for thinking through the choices to be made in structuring day-to-day life for children.

POVERTY IS PREVENTABLE. Because poverty threatens the well-being of *all* our children, there is no more important domestic public policy issue than shielding children from deprivation linked to poverty in the areas of health care, education, and so on. Use commitment to deal with childhood poverty as a litmus test for politicians who care about families and the future of America. If the rich get richer and the poor get poorer, our society will self-destruct as "the home of the free."

The Children's Defense Fund monitors politicians and their response to child poverty. Write to them at CDF, 25 E Street N.W., Washington, DC 20001.

Another resource is the National Center for Children in Poverty, Columbia University, School of Public Health, 154 Haven Avenue, New York, NY 10032.

QUALITY can apply to all we do. Self-esteem arises from pride in one's accomplishments as well as from a general sense of self-worth. Seeking excellence means setting high standards for children academically and socially—and also for political leaders, the marketplace, and ourselves. Once we accept that life is a challenge, we are on the quest for quality.

READ TO CHILDREN—any children you can reach. The development of literacy in children flows naturally when they live with adults who value the written word. Start in infancy and continue reading to children throughout childhood. Read for yourself as well. Literature offers both depth and breadth to children as they seek to make sense of the world. It grounds them in metaphor and myth, two useful tools in any civilization.

For suggestions on what and how to read for children see Betsy Hearne's book, *Choosing Books for Children*. You can also get advice from The National Center for Family Literacy, Dept. P, Waterfront Plaza, Suite 200, 325 West Main Street, Louisville, KY 40202–4251.

SCHOOLS SHOULD BE SMALL. Small high schools are the highest priority for detoxifying the social environment for adolescents. Bring this issue to the attention of school boards and legislators. The goal is legislation mandating a maximum size of 500 students in grades 9–12. The typical response is a bureaucratic division of a big school into several "schools within the school." This is not enough. Small schools have a complete program of extracurricular activities and a separate site that ensures that every single student is needed. Barker and Gump's *Big School, Small School* remains the classic resource on this issue.

Write to me and send a stamped, self-addressed envelope, and I'll send you an article summarizing the research and its implications. The address is James Garbarino, FLDC, G-20 MVR, Cornell University, Ithaca, NY 14853–4401.

TELEVISION IS A DRUG. Reduce the dosage by limiting children's exposure. One hour a day weekdays and two hours a day on weekends is plenty! Setting this and other standards stimulates decision-making discussions in the family. More than one TV in the house is a step in the wrong direction. See Marie Winn's books *The Plug-In Drug* and *Unplugging the Plug-In Drug* for useful guidance on how to deal with this particular drug abuse problem.

UNITE VALUES WITH ACTIONS. Values are just words if they aren't coupled with action. Values education builds character among children. Parents play a vital role by what they say and do, and by the way they support others who seek to develop the character of their children—teachers, clergy, friends of the family, and elders. Strong families have strong commitments to values beyond "have a nice day." Religious commitment, political activism, and community service all speak louder than words.

VIOLENCE PREVENTION STARTS AT HOME. Violence prevention strategies for detoxifying the social environment must start early for maximum effect. Parents can learn how to encourage a firm but gentle childrearing style from birth onward. Nonviolent discipline is the key to nonviolent children.

Murray Straus has put together all the existing evidence on why spanking and other forms of family violence are destructive in his book *Beating the Devil out of Them*.

In school, more formal programs can be designed to change the culture of violence in childhood. For an example, see *Let's Talk About Living in a World with Violence*, a workbook my colleagues and I developed for use with elementary school–aged children. For information, write the Family Life Development Center, G-20 MVR, Cornell University, Ithaca, NY 14853–4401.

For some guidance on dealing with violent toys, see *Who's Calling the Shots*, by Dr. Nancy Carlsson-Paige and Deborah Levin.

WALKING IS THE BEST WAY TO TRAVEL. It's good for the body and the spirit and is an ideal way for families to grow closer to each other and to their neighborhoods. If the distance to be traveled is a mile or less, walk it! Draw a map of your neighborhood and fill in the spaces before and after your walks. Who lives where? What are the landmarks? Where are the stores? Mapping is an excellent way to build social confidence in children—and adults. Walking fills in the human details. Many communities consider curfews a strategy for making things safer, but the real goal is not getting the kids off the street, but rather getting adults on the street.

XYLOPHONES ARE FUN! Simple fun is an important antidote to social toxicity. Playing music together in families and in community groups helps forge positive bonds of attachment. Once you turn off the TV, you'll have time to play games too. Monopoly, Scrabble, Candyland, Go Fish, Hearts, Rummy, and all the other *interactive* games of childhood are investments in the kind of childhood that increases your child's resistance to the forces of social toxicity.

YOU CAN CHANGE THE WORLD. Think it through, and plan first. What needs doing is not always obvious. Many people in the early 1950s bought television sets because they wanted to bring their families together. They changed the world, but not in the way they anticipated. Educational leaders in the 1960s argued for big high schools to increase educational offerings and create more efficient systems that would save money. They changed the world, but not for the better. SAT scores went down. Costs went up due to the social forces set loose in and by big schools. Alienation increased. The message is this: collect information; study the alternatives; think it through.

If you hear about simple solutions that seem too good to be true, they probably are too good to be true; don't trust the leaders who promote them. But don't simply blame others. The miraculous transformation we need must come from within as well as without each of us as a spiritual being capable of miracles. Read Wayne Dyer's *Real Magic* for guidance on how to proceed.

ZERO IN ON DEPERSONALIZATION, dehumanization, and desensitization. Identify every step that diminishes the humanity of any person and resist it. Empathy is the enemy of violence and nastiness. We all must refuse to dehumanize *anyone*. This soulful approach to the world is a foundation for efforts to detoxify our communal life. For guidance, see Thomas Moore's *Care of the Soul*.

Notes

Preface

1. Bronfenbrenner, 1970.

Chapter One

1. O'Neill has shown that while these kinds of historical differences are commonly cited, there is no clear empirical evidence to scientifically document them.
2. Entman, R., 1994, personal communication.
3. Miringoff, 1994.
4. Achenbach & Howell, 1993.
5. Garbarino, 1992c.
6. Carson, 1962.
7. Sameroff, Seifer, Barocas, Zax, & Greenspan, 1987; Dunst & Trivette, 1992.
8. Cohen & Naimark, 1990.
9. Korbin, 1992.
10. Getzels, 1974.
11. Finkelhor, 1979.
12. Montessori, 1967.
13. Bronowski, 1973.
14. Hoban, 1989.

15. Paley, 1983.

16. Elkind, 1980.

17. Johansson, 1984.

18. Blanc, 1994.

19. Elkind, 1985.

20. Winn, 1985.

21. Suransky, 1982.

22. O'Hara, 1962.

23. Straus & Gelles, 1990.

Chapter Two

1. Gump & Adelberg, 1978, p. 174.

2. Moos, 1979.

3. Barker & Gump, 1964.

4. Aldrich, 1979; Michelson & Roberts, 1979.

5. Aldous & Hill, 1969.

6. Elder, 1974.

7. Bronfenbrenner, 1979, p. 22.

8. Kohn, 1977.

9. Wallace, 1982.

10. de Lone, 1979, pp. 158–159.

11. Centerwall, 1989.

12. Joy, Kimball, & Zabrack, 1986.

13. U.S. Department of Justice, 1991; Jones & Krisberg, 1994.

14. American Psychological Association, 1993.

15. Albee, 1980.

16. Price & Desmond, 1987.

17. University of Michigan, 1993.

18. Garbarino, Guttmann, & Seeley, 1986.

Chapter Three

1. Gibran, 1969, p. 17.

2. Mangan, 1994.

3. Moran, 1994, p. 116.

4. Cherlin, 1981.

5. Duncan, 1994.

6. Richters & Martinez, 1993.

7. Mednick, 1988.

8. Friedan, 1974.

9. Stennet, Cherson, & DeFrain, 1979.

10. Garbarino, Guttman, & Seeley, 1986; Rohner, 1980.

11. For example, see Lewis, Beavers, Gossett, & Phillips, 1976.

12. Frost, 1949.

13. Mencken, 1929.

14. Daly, 1990.

15. Garbarino, Kostelny, & Dubrow, 1991.

16. Bronfenbrenner, 1986.

Chapter Four

1. Bell, 1991.

2. Growing up fast and frightened, *Newsweek*, 1993.

3. Harris & Associates, 1994.

4. "Growing up fast and frightened," *Newsweek*, 1993.

5. Stennet, Cherson, & DeFrain, 1979.

6. Lewis, Lovely, Yeager, & Femina, 1989.

7. Garbarino, Dubrow, Kostelny, & Pardo, 1992.

8. Chicago Police Department, 1993.

9. Heller, 1955.

10. Perry, 1994.

11. Papanek, 1972.

12. Osofsky, Wewers, Hann, & Fick, 1993.

13. Milgrim, 1965.

14. Terr, 1983.

15. Reiss & Roth, 1993.

16. Machiavelli, 1992 (originally published 1532).

17. Miller, 1984.

18. Dyer, 1992, p. 69.

19. Straus, 1994.

Chapter Five

1. Rohner, 1980.

2. Comer, 1988.

3. Comer, 1988, p. 45.

4. Maccoby, 1951, p. 428.

5. Winn, 1985.

6. Hamilton & Lawless, 1956.

7. Maccoby, 1951, p. 440.

8. Bronfenbrenner, 1970.

9. Barker & Gump, 1964.

10. Barker & Gump, 1964.

11. Barker & Gump, 1964.

12. Bureau of Justice Statistics, 1986.

Chapter Six

1. U.S. Census Bureau, 1992.

2. U.S. Census Bureau, 1992.

3. Steinberg & Dornbusch, 1991.

4. Stout, 1983.

5. Achenbach & Howell, 1993.

6. Reppucci, 1983.

7. Elkind, 1985.

8. Arthur, 1983.

9. Bahr, 1978.

10. Duncan, 1994.

11. Richardson and others, 1989.

12. Pressor, 1984.

13. Cherlin, 1981.

14. Suransky, 1982.

15. Gilkerson, Nesphachel, & Trevino, 1987.

16. Cleary, 1981, 1984.

Chapter Seven

1. Garbarino, 1992c.

2. Vygotsky, 1986.

3. Gilligan, 1982.

4. Erdley & Asher, 1993.

5. Erikson, 1976.

6. Coulton & Pandey, 1992.

7. Joy, Kimball, & Zabrack, 1986.

Chapter Eight

1. Korbin, 1992.

2. Bane & Ellwood, 1989.

3. Fonseka & Malhortora, 1994.

4. Center on Budget and Policy Priorities, 1989.

5. Garbarino, 1992b.

6. Economic Policy Institute, 1989.

7. U.S. Census Bureau, 1989.

8. Wilson, 1987.

9. Miller, 1987.

10. Bronfenbrenner, 1986.

11. Garbarino, 1981.

12. Garbarino, 1992a.

Chapter Nine

1. Sameroff, Seifer, Barocas, Zax, & Greenspan, 1987.

2. Sameroff, Seifer, Barocas, Zax, & Greenspan, 1987.

3. Rutter, 1989.

4. Sameroff, Seifer, Barocas, Zax, & Greenspan, 1987.

5. Dunst & Trivette, 1992.

6. Center on Addiction and Substance Abuse, 1994.

7. Bronfenbrenner, 1986.

8. Willerman, Broman, & Fiedler, 1972.

9. Coles, 1986.

10. Wallerstein & Kelly, 1989.

11. Caspi, 1989; Elder & Rockwell, 1978.

12. Scheinfeld, 1983.

13. Losel & Bliesener, 1990.

14. Rutter, 1989.

15. Bronfenbrenner, 1970.

16. Carson, 1962.

17. Bettelheim & Rosenfeld, 1992, p. 192.

References

Achenbach, T., & Howell, C. (1993). Are American children's problems getting worse? A thirteen-year comparison. *Journal of the American Academy of Child and Adolescent Psychiatry, 32*(6), 1145–1154.

Albee, G. (1980). Primary prevention and social problems. In G. Gerbner, C. Ross, & E. Zigler (Eds.), *Child abuse: An agenda for action,* (pp. 106–117). New York: Oxford University Press.

Aldous, J., & Hill, R. (1969). Breaking the poverty cycle: Strategic points for intervention. *Social Work, 14,* 3–12.

Aldrich, R. (1979). The influences of man-built environment on children and youth. In W. Michelson, S. Levine, & E. Michelson (Eds.), *The child in the city, Vol. 1.* Toronto: University of Toronto Press.

American Psychological Association. (1993). *Summary Report of the American Psychological Association Commission on Violence and Youth: Vol. I. Violence and youth: Psychology's response.* Washington, DC: Author.

Arthur, H. (1983). The Japan gap. *American Educator, 10*: 38–44.

Bahr, H. (1978, August). *Change in family life in Middletown: 1924–1977.* Paper presented at the annual meeting of the American Sociological Association, Chicago.

Bane, M., and Ellwood, D. (1989). Slipping into and out of poverty: The dynamics of spells. Cambridge, MA: National Bureau of Economic Research.

Barker, R., & Gump, P. (1964). *Big school, small school.* Stanford, CA: Stanford University Press.

Bell, C. (1991). Traumatic stress and children in danger. *Journal of Health Care for the Poor and Underserved, 2*(1), 175–188.

Bettelheim, B., & Rosenfeld, A. A. (1992). *The art of the obvious: Developing insight for psychotherapy and everyday life.* New York: Knopf.

Blanc, C. (1994). *Urban children in distress: Global predicaments and innovative strategies.* Langhorn, PA: Gordon and Beach Science Publishers.

Bronfenbrenner, U. (1970). *Two worlds of childhood.* New York: Russell Sage Foundation.

Bronfenbrenner, U. (1979). *The ecology of human development: Experiments by nature and design.* Cambridge, MA: Harvard University Press.

Bronfenbrenner, U. (1986). Ecology of the family as a context for human development research perspectives. *Developmental Psychology, 22,* 723–742.

Bronowski, J. (1973). *The ascent of man.* Boston: Little, Brown.

Bureau of Justice Statistics, U.S. Department of Justice. (1986). *School crime.* Washington, DC: U.S. Government Printing Office.

Carlsson-Paige, N., & Levin, D. E. (1990). *Who's calling the shots?* Philadelphia: New Society.

Carson, R. (1962). *Silent spring.* New York: Houghton-Mifflin.

Caspi, A. (1989). Continuities and consequences of interactional styles across the life course. *Journal of Personality, 57,* 375–406.

Center on Addiction and Substance Abuse. (1994). Substance abuse and women on welfare. New York: Center on Addiction and Substance Abuse at Columbia University.

Center on Budget and Policy Priorities. (1989). *Low income housing: Data from the American Housing Survey.* Washington, DC: Author.

Centerwall, B. S. (1989). Exposure to television as a cause of violence. In G. Comstock (Ed.), *Public communication and behavior, Vol. 2.* (pp. 1–58). Orlando, FL: Academic Press.

Cherlin, A. (1981). *Marriage, divorce, remarriage: Changing patterns in the postwar United States.* Cambridge, MA: Harvard University Press.

Chicago Police Department. (1993). *Chicago Police Department murder analysis report.* Chicago: Author.

Cleary, B. (1981). *Ramona Quimby: Age 8.* New York: Bantam Doubleday Dell.

Cleary, B. (1984). *Ramona forever.* New York: Morrow Jr. Books.

Cohen, C. & Naimark, H. (1991). United Nations Convention on the Rights of the Child: Individual rights concepts and their significance for social scientists. *American Psychologist, 46,* 60–65.

Coles, R. (1986). *The political life of children.* Boston: Houghton Mifflin.

Comer, J. (1988). *Maggie's American dream: The life and times of a black family.* New York: Penguin.

Coolsen, P., Seligson, M., & Garbarino, J. (1985). *When school's out and nobody's home.* Chicago: National Committee for Prevention of Child Abuse.

Coulton, C., & Pandey, S. (1992). Geographic concentration of poverty and risk to children in urban neighborhoods. *American Behavioral Scientist, 35,* 238–257.

Daly, M. (1990). The true meaning of "home." In *The Better Homes Foundation 1989 Annual Report.* Boston: The Better Homes Foundation.

de Lone, R. (1979). *Small futures: Children, inequality, and the limits of liberal reform.* Orlando, FL: Harcourt Brace Jovanovich.

Duncan, S. (1994). Economic impact of divorce on childhood development: Current findings and policy implications. *Journal of Clinical Psychology*, 23, 444–457.

Dunst, C. J., & Trivette, C. M. (1992). *Risk and opportunity factors influencing parent and child functioning*. Paper based upon presentations made at the Ninth Annual Smoky Mountain Winter Institute, Ashville, NC.

Dyer, W. R. (1992). *Real magic: Creating miracles in everyday life*. New York: HarperCollins.

Economic Policy Institute. (1989). *The state of working America*. Washington, DC: Author.

Elder, G. (1974). *Children of the Great Depression: Social change in life experience*. Chicago: University of Chicago Press.

Elder, G., & Rockwell, R. (1978). *The life course and human development: An ecological perspective*. Unpublished manuscript. Boys Town, NE: Boys Town Center for the Study of Youth Development.

Elkind, D. (1980). Strategic interactions. In J. Adelson (Ed.) *Handbook of Adolescent Psychology*. New Brunswick, NJ: Transaction.

Elkind, D. (1985). *The hurried child*. Reading, MA: Addison-Wesley.

Erdley, C., & Asher, S. (1993). *Linkages between children's beliefs about the legitimacy of aggression and their behavior*. Urbana: University of Illinois at Urbana.

Erikson, K. (1976). *Everything in its path: Destruction of community in the Buffalo Creek flood*. New York: Simon & Schuster.

Finkelhor, D. (1979). *Sexually victimized children*. New York: Free Press.

Fonseka, L., & Malhortora, D. (1994). India: Urban poverty, children and participation. In C. Blanc (Ed.), *Urban children in distress*. Langhorne, PA: Gordon and Breach.

Friedan, B. (1974). *The feminine mystique*. New York: W. W. Norton.

Frost, R. (1949). The death of a hired hand. In *Complete poems of Robert Frost*. Troy, MO: Holt, Rinehart & Winston.

Garbarino, J. (1981). *Successful schools and competent students*. Lexington, MA: Lexington Books.

Garbarino, J. (1992a). *Children and families in the social environment* (2nd ed.). New York: Aldine.

Garbarino, J. (1992b). The meaning of poverty to children. *American Behavioral Scientist*, 35, 220–237.

Garbarino, J. (1992c). *Toward a sustainable society*. Chicago: Noble Press.

Garbarino, J., Dubrow, N., Kostelny, K., and Pardo, C. (1992). *Children in danger: Coping with the consequences of community violence*. San Francisco: Jossey-Bass.

Garbarino, J., Guttmann, E., & Seeley, J. W. (1986). *The psychologically battered child: Strategies for identification, assessment, and intervention.* San Francisco: Jossey-Bass.

Garbarino, J., Kostelny, K., & Dubrow, N. (1991). *No place to be a child: Growing up in a war zone.* Lexington, MA: Lexington Books.

Getzels, J. (1974). Socialization and education: A note on discontinuities. *Teacher's College Record, 76,* 218–225.

Gibran, K. (1969). *The prophet.* New York: Knopf. (Original work published 1923)

Gilkerson, L., Nesphachel, S., & Trevino, R. (1987) *Issues in family day care.* Chicago: Erikson Institute.

Gilligan, C. (1982). *In a different voice.* Cambridge, MA: Harvard University Press.

Growing up fast and frightened. (1993, November 22). *Newsweek,* pp. 52–53.

Gump, P., & Adelberg, B. (1978). Urbanism from the perspective of ecological psychologists. *Environment and Behavior, 10,* 171–191.

Hamilton, R., & Lawless, R. (1956). Television within the social matrix. *Public Opinion Quarterly, 20,* 393–403.

Harris & Associates. (1994). *Metropolitan Life survey of the American teacher: Violence in America's public schools, Part II.* Metropolitan Life Insurance.

Hearne, B. (1992). *Choosing books for children: A common sense guide.* (2nd ed.). New York: Delacorte.

Heller, J. (1989). *Catch 22.* New York: Dell. (Original work published 1955)

Hoban, R. (1989). *How Tom beat Captain Narjork and his hired sportsmen.* Minneapolis: Lerner.

Johansson, S. R. (1984, May). *Neglect, abuse, and avoidable death.* Paper presented to a conference on Child Abuse: A Bio-Social Perspective, convened by the Social Science Research Council, New York.

Jones, M., & Krisberg, B. (1994). *Images and reality: Juvenile crime, youth violence and public policy.* San Francisco: National Council on Crime and Delinquency.

Joy, L. A., Kimball, M. M., & Zabrack, M. L. (1986). Television and children's aggressive behavior. In *The impact of television: A natural experiment in three communities* (pp. 303–360). Orlando, FL: Academic Press.

Kohn, M. (1977). *Class and conformity: A study in values* (2nd ed.). Chicago: University of Chicago Press.

Korbin, J. (1992). Introduction: Child poverty in the U.S. *The American Behavioral Scientist, 35,* 213–219.

Lewis, D., Lovely, R., Yeager, C., & Femina, D. (1989). Toward a theory of the genesis of violence: A follow-up study of delinquents. *American Journal of Child and Adolescent Psychiatry, 28,* 431–436.

Lewis, J., Beavers, W., Gossett, J., & Phillips, V. (1976). *No single thread: Psychological health in family systems*. New York: Brunner/Mazel.

Losel, F., & Bliesener, T. (1990). Resilience in adolescence: A study on the generalizability of protective factors. In K. Hurrelmann & F. Losel (Eds.), *Health hazards in adolescence*. New York: Walter de Gruyter.

Maccoby, E. (1951) Television: Its impact on school children. *Public Opinion Quarterly, 15*, 423–444.

Machiavelli, N. (1992). *The prince*. New York: W. W. Norton. (Original work published 1532)

Mangan, J. (1994, January 2). Vintage sitcoms give kids a reality check. *Chicago Tribune, TV Guide*, p. 5.

Mednick, S. (1988). *Biological bases of antisocial behavior*. Norwell, MA: Kluwer.

Mencken, H. L. (1929). Cited in *I'll invest my money in people*. Battlecreek, MI: W. F. Kellogg Foundation, 1990.

Michelson, W., & Roberts, E. (1979). Children and the urban physical environment. In W. Michelson, S. Levine, & A. Spina (Eds.), *The child in the city, Vol. 2*. Toronto: University of Toronto Press.

Milgrim, S. (1965). Some conditions of obedience and disobedience to authority. *Human Relations, 18*, 57–75.

Miller, A. (1984). *Thou shalt not be aware: Society's betrayal of the child*. New York: Farrar, Straus & Giroux.

Miller, A. (1987). *Maternal health and infant survival: An analysis of medical and social services to pregnant women, newborns, and their families in ten European countries*. Washington, DC: National Center for Clinical Infant Programs.

Miringoff, M. (1994). *Monitoring the social well-being of the nation: The index of social health*. Tarrytown, NY: Fordham Institute for Social Policy.

Montessori, M. (1967). *The absorbent mind*. New York: Dell.

Moore, T. (1992). *Care of the soul*. New York: HarperCollins.

Moos, R. (1979). *Evaluating educational environments: Procedures, measures, findings and policy implications*. San Francisco: Jossey-Bass.

Moran, S. (1994). Creative reading: Books in the classroom. *Horn, 70*, 115–118.

O'Hara, R. (1962). The roots of career. *Elementary School Journal, 62*, 277–280.

Osofsky, J., Wewers, S., Hann, D., & Fick, A. (1993). Chronic community violence: What is happening to our children? *Psychiatry, 56*, 36–45.

Paley, V. (1983). *Wally's stories: Conversations in the kindergarten*. Cambridge, MA: Harvard University Press.

Paley, V. (1984). *Boys and girls: Superheroes in the doll corner*. Chicago: University of Chicago Press.

Paley, V. (1988). *Bad guys don't have birthdays: Fantasy play at four.* Chicago: University of Chicago Press.

Paley, V. (1992). *You can't say you can't play.* Cambridge, MA: Harvard University Press.

Papanek, V. (1972). Design for the real world: Human ecology and social change. New York: Pantheon Books.

Perry, B. (1994, March). *Children of Waco.* Presentation to the Chicago Association for Child and Adolescent Psychiatry.

Pressor, H. (1984). Work and family. Colloquium presentation, The Pennsylvania State University.

Price, J. & Desmond, S. (1987). The missing children issue: A preliminary examination of fifth-grade students' perceptions. *American Journal of Diseases of Children, 141,* 811–815.

Reiss, A. and Roth, J. (1993). Understanding and preventing violence. Washington, D.C.: National Academy Press.

Reppucci, D. (1983, August). *Emerging issues in the ecology of children and families.* Invited address to the 91st annual meeting, American Psychological Association, Anaheim, CA.

Richardson, J., Dwyer, K., McGuigan, K., Hansen, W., Dent, C., Johnson, C., Sussman, S., Brannon, B., & Flay, B. (1989). Substance use among eighth-grade students who take care of themselves after school. *Pediatrics, 84,* 556–566.

Richters, J., & Martinez, P. (1993). The NIMH community violence project: Children's distress symptoms associated with violence exposure. *Psychiatry, 56,* 22–35.

Rohner, R. (1980). Worldwide tests of parental acceptance-rejection theory: An overview. *Behavior Science Research, 15,* 1–21.

Rutter, M. (1989). Pathways from childhood to adult life. *Journal of Psychology and Psychiatry, 30,* 23–51.

Sameroff, A., Seifer, R., Barocas, R., Zax, M., & Greenspan, S. (1987). Intelligence quotient scores of 4-year-old children: Social-environmental risk factors. *Pediatrics, 79,* 343–350.

Scheinfeld, D. (1983, January). Family relationships and school achievement among boys of lower-income urban black families. *American Journal of Orthopsychiatry, 53*(1), 127–143.

Steinberg, L. & Dornbusch, S. (1991). Negative correlates of part-time employment during adolescence: Replication and elaboration. *Developmental Psychology, 27,* 304–313.

Stennet, N., Chersen, B., & DeFrain, J. (1979). *Building family strength.* Ann Arbor, MI: Books on Demand.

Stout, K. (1983, October). Bringing up better babies. *Mainliver Magazine,* 132.

Straus, M. (1994). *Beating the devil out of them: Corporal punishment in American families*. Lexington, MA: Free Press.

Straus, M., & Gelles, R. (1990). *Physical violence in American families: Risk factors and adaptations to violence in 8,145 families*. New Brunswick, NJ: Transaction.

Suransky, V. (1982). *The erosion of childhood*. Chicago: University of Chicago Press.

Terr, L. (1983). Chowchilla revisited: The effects of psychic trauma four years after a school-bus kidnapping. *American Journal of Psychiatry, 140,* 1543–1550.

University of Michigan. (1993). *Monitoring the future 1975–1992*. Ann Arbor, MI: Author.

U.S. Census Bureau. (1989). *Money, income and poverty studies of families and persons in the United States* (Current Population Reports, Series P-60, No. 166). Washington, DC: U.S. Department of Commerce.

U.S. Census Bureau. (1992). *Current population reports*. Washington, DC: U.S. Government Printing Office.

U.S. Department of Justice, Office of Juvenile Justice and Delinquency Prevention. (1991). *Children in custody: Public juvenile facilities*. Washington, DC: U.S. Government Printing Office.

Vygotsky, L. (1986). *Thought and language*. Cambridge, MA: MIT Press.

Wallace, R. (1982). The New York City fire epidemic as a toxic phenomenon. *International Archives of Occupational and Environmental Health, 50,* 33.

Wallerstein, J. S., & Kelly, J. B. (1989). *Surviving the breakup: How children and parents cope with divorce*. New York: Basic Books.

Willerman, L., Broman, S., & Fiedler, M. (1972). Infant development, preschool IQ and social class. *Child Development, 41,* 69–77.

Wilson, W. (1987). The truly disadvantaged: The inner city, the underclass, and public policy. Chicago: University of Chicago Press.

Winn, M. (1985). *The plug-in drug: Television, children and the family*. New York: Viking Penguin.

Winn, M. (1987). *Unplugging the plug-in drug*. New York: Viking Penguin.

Zigler, E. (1986). The "gourmet baby" and the "little wildflower." *Zero to Three, 7*(2), 8–12.

Index

Carson, R., 4, 163
Catch-22 (Heller), 76–77
CBS News, 112
Census Bureau, 65
Cherlin, A., 46
Chicago, Ill., 75–76
Chicago Tribune, 43
Child abuse, 1; and discipline, 87–88; neurological damage from, 68; possibility of, 82; prevalence of, 19; protection from, 10–11; and psychological maltreatment, 39; and violent children, 68, 69–71. *See also* Domestic Violence; Violence
Child Behavior Checklist, 2–3
Child care: by children, 115–116; consistency in, 58–59, 60; externalizing costs of, 107–109; in monetarized versus nonmonetarized economies, 103–104, 107–109, 114–119, 139; quality of, 117–118; staff-child ratios in, 117–118
Child development: cognitive, 151–155; complexity of, 47; and coping skills, 155–158; effects of violent trauma on, 77–78, 82–84; and gender, 165–166; and identity creation, 89–100; moral, 124–125, 156, 162–163; and opportunity, 153–155; and poverty, 136, 144; as purpose of family, 52–53; and resilience, 158–164; and risk accumulation, 151–155; and security, 63; social influences on, 154–155; social map framework of, 23–32
Child support, 62, 116
Childhood: ecology of, 30–32; economy of time in, 102, 109–114; global consensus on, 7–10; length of, 12, 14–15, 109–114; meaning of, 6–11, 15–17, 32; protected, 8–10, 15–17; protected, erosion of, 16–17, 30–32, 35–37; purpose of, 12–15; stages of, and family change, 56–58, 61–62
Childrearing: affirmation and acceptance in, 89–100; community and, 126–131; complexity of, 47; economics and, 135–148; educating parents for, 61; family stability and, 41–62; financial costs of, 119, 140–141; as human capital investment, 101–109, 110–114; in 1950s versus 1990s, 17–20, 43–45; nonviolent, 10, 87–88, 157–158, 172; resources for, 165–173; rewards of,

104, 119; security and, 63–88; as a social act, 126–127; stresses of, 53, 158; time and, 101–120; values and, 121–126
Children: as first priority, 166; increase in emotional/behavioral problems of, 1–6; needs of, for a home, 56–58; physical fitness of, 19, 122; powerless of, 36–37; rights of, 8–10; self-care by, 115–119; temperaments of, 59, 160–161; in therapy, 3; vulnerability of, 5–6, 61. *See also* Behavioral/emotional problems; Risk factors; Vulnerability
"Children of War," 85–86
Children's Defense Fund, 64, 170
Choosing Books for Children (Hearne), 170
Chorn, A., 85–86
Churches, 49
Cleary, B., 118
Clothing, adult versus child, 10–11
Cognitive development: and resilience, 159; and risk accumulation, 151–155
Coles, R., 156
Comer, J., 90–91
Commitment: to children, 166; family, 55, 122–123; of parents, 114; and values, 171
Communication patterns, within families, 54–55
Community: and child care, 107–109; connecting with, 126–131; and creating security, 88; and creating stability, 60–62; economic diversity within, 128–129, 132, 168; and economic justice, 133; effects of fear on, 130–131; effects of television on, 129–130; and moral development, 124–125; participation in, 132, 160; responsibilities of, 20–21, 49–50, 126–133, 162–164; role of, in fostering resilience, 161–162; schools and, 99; strategies for strengthening, 131–133; walking in the, 172
Commuting, 105
Competence: and adult leadership, 124–125; development of, 13–14; and play, 14–15; and self-esteem, 54; and success, 159–160
Competition, academic, 111–112
Complexity: of child-environment relationship, 28–30; of child-family rela-